USING XML

A How-To-Do-It Manual® and CD-ROM for Librarians

KWONG BOR NG

HOW-TO-DO-IT MANUALS

NUMBER 154

NEAL-SCHUMAN PUBLISHERS, INC.
New York London

Published by Neal-Schuman Publishers, Inc.
100 William St., Suite 2004
New York, NY 10038

Printed and bound in the United States of America.

The paper used in this publication meets the minimum requirements of American National Standard for Information Sciences—Permanence of Paper for Printed Library Materials, ANSI Z39.48-1992.

ISBN-13: 978-1-55570-567-1
ISBN-10: 1-55570-567-7

Library of Congress Cataloging-in-Publication Data

Ng, Kwong Bor.
Using XML : a how-to-do-it manual and CD-ROM for librarians / by Kwong Bor Ng.
p. cm. — (How-to-do-it manuals ; no. 154)
Includes bibliographical references and index.
ISBN 978-1-55570-567-1 (alk. paper)
1. XML (Document markup language). 2. Cataloging—Data processing. 3. Machine-readable bibliographic data formats. 4. Metadata. I. Title.
Z678.93.X54N48 2007
006.7'4—dc22

2007008089

CONTENTS

LIST OF FIGURES

LIST OF EXERCISES

PREFACE

The acronym XML stands for eXtensible Markup Language, today's standard method of presenting content on the Web and in other online arenas. This amazingly versatile language has many library applications.

Before opening these pages, you may have already tried to learn XML by following free online tutorials or reading general introductory texts. Though the explanations may make sense in theory, they don't address libraries' specialized needs. Applying the knowledge you glean from simple tutorials to tasks such as creating a catalog record may not work. Why not? Because in the real world, you must take into account library-specific constraints. For instance, the Machine Readable Catalog Record (MARC) format has its own data structure, which nonlibrary sources do not explain. Learning XML is not difficult, but you must start with the proper tools. I designed *Using XML: A How-To-Do-It Manual for Librarians* as an introductory resource specific to libraries.

Once you recognize what XML looks like, you'll quickly see that it's already present in databases, catalogs, indexes, and other tools that you and your patrons consult daily. XML also underlies many interlibrary loan, Web design, and digital library applications. In any of these areas, XML knowledge can make tasks easier. It can handle the special characters and non-Roman scripts often found in bibliographic records. For digital libraries and archival systems, it also offers the greatest promise of data longevity. Technical services librarians, metadata librarians, system librarians, and Webmasters will particularly benefit from XML knowledge.

After reading these pages and completing the exercises, you will have a fundamental education in XML-based resource description and bibliographic data management. Using XML covers general XML syntax; explains schema language, which allows you to impose a predetermined structure on a document; and introduces presentational language for content display and delivery. You will also discover multiple vocabulary schemes and practice applying auxiliary technologies to existing standards.

Step-by-step examples illustrate XML principles. Work all the exercises in order, without skipping, so you don't miss important concepts. You can easily check your work using the CD-ROM, which reproduces the examples.

ORGANIZATION

Part I, "Introducing XML," covers the basics of the language and its primary uses.

- Chapter 1, "What is XML?" explains the concept of markup languages and XML's developmental history.
- Chapter 2, "XML Applications in Libraries," summarizes the most common functions, including text collections encoding, automation, digital libraries, and technical services.

In Part II, "Basic XML Techniques," tutorials help you develop your own documents.

- Chapter 3, "Creating and Organizing an XML Document," focuses on the basic document's building blocks, covering prologs and declaration, elements, naming, comments, and attributes.
- In Chapter 4, "Processing an XML Document," shows how to create special characters, skip data, define entities, and use entity reference.
- Chapter 5, "Viewing XML Documents: Using Cascading Style Sheets (CSS)," discusses the rules and syntax of CSS, displaying a document on the Web, and when and why to use a style sheet.

Part III, "Intermediate XML Techniques," explains Document Type Declaration (DTD).

- Chapter 6, "Assigning Structure Using Document Type Declarations and Document Type Definitions," covers the basics of defining document structure through several exercises.
- Chapter 7, "Structuring an XML Document Using Attribute List Declarations and Entity Declarations," outlines attribute list declaration and entity declaration; provides a short introduction to MARC DTD (discussed further in Appendices 1 and 2) and defines validity in an XML document.
- Chapter 8, "Namespaces and Limitations of DTD," identifies ways to correct for the format's weaknesses. Other

topics include the Dublin Core Metadata Element Set (DCMES), the use of DCMES DTD to create a catalog record, and the legal scope of names.

In Part IV, "Advanced XML Techniques," you will take your knowledge to the next level using schema language and Extensible Stylesheet Language.

- Chapter 9, "Assigning Structure to an XML Document Using W3C XML Schema Language," addresses another way of defining document attributes. You will also learn how to convert documents from using DTD to using schema.
- Chapter 10, "Transforming XML Documents Using Extensible Stylesheet Language," shows how to deliver XML documents through the Web and create a clean and pleasing document display using Internet Explorer.

Three appendices provide additional reference information. Appendices 1 and 2 cover a DTD and a slim schema of MARC. Appendix 3 defines basic XML terms.

HOW TO USE THE CD-ROM

The CD-ROM includes complete copies of all the in-chapter exercises. (The book abbreviates some longer exercises.) If your document does not display properly, compare your work to the CD-ROM example. The CD also holds several documents originally published by W3C. Refer to these if you want more information about a W3C standard or protocol.

Current trends suggest that XML use, already ubiquitous, will continue to expand, making XML knowledge one of today's most important technical skills for librarians. XML's inherent flexibility means that it will evolve constantly and new approaches will regularly emerge. Understanding XML fundamentals will help you adapt so your library can use XML to the greatest advantage for many years to come.

1 INTRODUCING XML

1 WHAT IS XML?

MARKUP LANGUAGES

XML stands for eXtensible Markup Language. Many markup languages exist, and they all have the same fundamental purpose: to take bits of text and describe their components. In this sense, using a markup language is much like diagramming a sentence: each approach takes a careful look at all elements in a sentence (or a string of text, in programming-speak) and adds descriptive notations. In a sentence diagram, those notations are indicated with lines; in a markup language, those notations are indicated with tags. In both cases, the idea is to describe exactly what each element of a string is and exactly how it relates to the others.

For example, a paragraph of plain text may look like this:

```
I love my orange tulip. I hate your sour green orange.
```

The first occurrence of the word "orange" refers to a color, while the second refers to a fruit. If we are to freely use the word "orange" in both these senses, we need to be clear about precisely what it means in each instance. Using a markup language, we can specify the nature of each significant element of this paragraph simply by tagging it:

```
<color> orange </color>
<fruit> orange </fruit>
```

This way, even a creature as literal minded as a computer will know exactly what we mean by "orange" when it appears in our paragraph.

The process of inserting markup tags is called text encoding. Adding markup tags does not change the meaning of the paragraph; it simply allows us to easily identify its components. After encoding, the paragraph has a structure described by the markup tags, much like a diagram describes a sentence's grammatical structure. In fact, we can encode our entire sample paragraph to specify its parts of speech:

```
<paragraph>
   <sentence>
      <subject> I </subject>
      <verb> love </verb>
      <possessive> my </possessive>
      <adjective> orange </adjective>
      <object> tulip </object>
   </sentence>
   <sentence>
      <subject> I </subject>
      <verb> hate </verb>
      <possessive> your </possessive>
      <adjective> sour </adjective>
      <adjective> green </adjective>
      <object> orange </object>
   </sentence>
</paragraph>
```

Notice that we have tagged each word *and* each logical unit—paragraph, sentences—of our text. Tags can contain tags just as paragraphs contain sentences; this is known as nesting. The addition of the tags doesn't change the meaning of the paragraph, but the tags add a structure to the text that enables different grammatical components to be identified and processed appropriately.

In the previous example, we worked from a given structure—English grammar—and tagged our paragraph accordingly. But what if we want to organize things differently, in a way that speaks more directly to the way we plan to use the data we're tagging? Generalized markup languages allow us to define and use our own customized tags.

In our example, each sentence expresses an opinion, which we can identify by creating an <opinion> tag. Each opinion expresses a disposition, which we can tag, toward an object... but we don't have to be so formal when we tag that part; we can call it a "doodad" if we like, resulting in something like this:

```
<paragraph>
   <sentence>
```

```
        <opinion>
            <subject> I </subject>
            <disposition> love </disposition>
            <possessive> my </possessive>
            <doodad>
                <color> orange </color>
                <flower> tulip </flower>
            </doodad>
        </opinion>
    </sentence>
    <sentence>
        <opinion>
            <subject> I </subject>
            <disposition> hate </disposition>
            <possessive> your </ possessive>
            <doodad>
                <taste> sour </taste>
                <color> green </color>
                <fruit> orange </fruit>
            </doodad>
        </opinion>
    </sentence> .
</paragraph>
```

In essence, our document is now described using a new markup language: one of dispositions and doodads rather than verbs and objects.

In the real world, new markup languages are constantly being developed to meet specific needs. The most widely used markup language is HTML (Hypertext Markup Language), which uses tags to identify Web page components so that a Web browser can display the page properly: for instance, <h1>...</h1> describes a level-one heading, <p>...</p> indicates a paragraph, and <a>...</a> identifies an anchor. Beyond HTML, SVG (Scalable Vector Graphics) is a markup language for describing two-dimensional graphics, EAD (Encoded Archival Description) is a long-standing tool for describing archival holdings, and NewsML (News Markup Language) is a markup language for global news exchange.

Specific markup languages can be developed to meet specific needs. SVG, for instance, describes graphics, while EAD focuses on archival holdings. Despite their different applications, a glance at the snippets below shows that the two languages bear some striking similarities due to their common parentage.

SVG (Scalable Vector Graphics)

```
<svg width="100%" height="100%" version="1.1"
xmlns="http://www.me.org/namespaces/svg">
    <ellipse cx="210" cy="150" rx="290" ry="20"
style="fill:black"/>
    <ellipse cx="180" cy="90" rx="165" ry="32"
style="fill:red"/>
    <ellipse cx="190" cy="22" rx="230" ry="65"
style="fill:blue"/>
</svg>
```

EAD (Encoded Archival Description)

```
<ead id="ns6784">
    <eadheader audience="internal" langencoding=
"ISO639-2" findaidstatus="edited-full-draft">
    <eadid type="SGML catalog">PUBLIC
"-//University of Me::Library::University Archives//TEXT
(US::NSU:: ns6784::Al Chu Papers)//EN" "ns6784.xml"
</eadid>
    <filedesc>
        <titlestmt>
        <titleproper>The Al Chu Papers<date>
c.1954-2006</date>
        </titleproper>
</titlestmt>
</filedesc>
</eadheader>
</ead>
```

Figure 1-1: Markup Languages: Examples

XML is also a markup language that uses tags to encode text in order to add a meaningful structure that computers (and humans) can understand and use. However, unlike HTML or SVG, which are markup languages developed for specific tasks, XML is a general-purpose markup language. Technically, there is almost no limitation on the purposes and kinds of text you can encode with XML. In fact, many special-purpose markup languages were developed and formalized using XML. In other words, XML is not just a markup language but also a meta-language: a language used to make statements about another language. For example, if you used English to describe or specify the vocabulary and grammar of Pig Latin, you would be using English as a meta-language. In other words, you can use XML to create your own markup language to encode exactly the types of documents that are important to you.

This means that XML itself has no predefined markup tags. Using XML, you define your own set of markup tags and the structural relationships between them to create a new markup language. The formal specification of this new language—its vocabulary and grammar—is described, or formalized, using a Document Type Definition (DTD), or an XML Schema. For instance, the latest versions of HTML were created and formalized in XML using a set of DTDs.

Many knowledge communities have developed their own markup languages in XML. In the library world, one of the most prominent XML-based languages is MODS (Metadata Object Description Schema), which is used to encode selected data from MARC records as well as other resource description records. A catalog record encoded in MODS is an XML document; the components of the record are identified by markup tags. The rules defining each tag and the structural relationships among them are formalized using XML Schema.

You will learn more about XML DTD in Chapters 6 and 7. You will learn more about XML Schema in Chapter 9.

FROM GML AND SGML TO XML

XML is relatively new on the scene, even by digital-technology standards. The first stable version of XML became a World Wide Web Consortium (W3C) recommendation in 1998. The latest version is version 1.1, which became a W3C recommendation in 2004. Before XML was developed, the dominant markup language was SGML (Standard Generalized Markup Language), which can be considered the "parent" of XML. In fact, many XML-based markup languages (MARCXML, TEI, etc.) commonly used in the knowledge community were originally implemented in SGML. To understand where XML came from and why it was developed, we need to look back to SGML.

W3C is an international organization overseeing the creation and promotion of Web standards and guidelines.

The concept of using generic descriptive tags to encode documents was first developed and used in publishing and printing industries in the 1960s. The basic goal then, as it is now, was to separate informational content from its presentation, so that each could be modified freely and flexibly. In 1969, IBM invented the Generalized Markup Language (GML), which introduced the idea of different grammar specifications for different kinds of documents. This concept laid the groundwork for GML's evolution into a meta-language. The use of tags like <fruit>. . . </fruit> and <color>. . . </color> for component identification was also introduced in GML. In 1978, the American National Standards Institute (ANSI) Committee on Information Processing established a separate committee charged with the task of developing a national standard for generic markup language based on GML; this standard later evolved into SGML (Standard Generalized Markup Language). SGML became an international standard in 1985, with the endorsement of the International Organization for Standardization (ISO). With international recognition, SGML was widely adopted by U.S. government agencies, public contractors, large manufacturing companies, technical information publishers, and other organizations.

ANSI and ISO are the two most important standards-establishing organizations for developers working in the U.S. market.

SGML is a broadly applicable, general-purpose markup language. It is also a meta-language that can be used to create new markup languages focused on specific tasks. Before XML's debut, most special-purpose markup languages—HTML, for instance—were created using SGML.

SGML is very powerful, but also very complicated and difficult to learn. By the mid-1990s, another working group was formed under the auspice of the W3C. Its task was to simplify SGML, creating a new general-purpose markup language that offered 80% of SGML's power at 20% of its complexity. The result was XML.

> A W3C Recommendation is a specification or set of guidelines that has received the endorsement of the W3C's members and director. It has roughly the same weight as an international protocol or standard.

The first version of XML became a W3C recommendation on February 10, 1998. It was enthusiastically received: organizations quickly began changing over from SGML. For example, in the mid-1990s, the Library of Congress' Network Development and MARC Standards Office developed two SGML DTDs that supported the conversion of cataloging data from MARC to SGML and back again without loss of data. Later, the SGML DTDs were converted to XML DTDs.

GROWTH OF THE XML FAMILY

As more and more organizations and institutions pick up XML, new standards are developed to address new needs and opportunities. Important additions include XML Schema Language, namespaces, Extensible Stylesheet Language (XSL) and XML Path Language (XPath).

Namespaces in XML: In an earlier example, we used tags to clarify what we meant by the word "orange" when it appeared in different contexts. But what if we wish to use the same tag in different ways? Say we'd like to use a <title> tag to describe both a book's title and the professional title used by its author. XML namespaces provide a simple method for qualifying XML element names and XML attribute names. For instance, in one XML namespace, the <title>...</title> tag may be used to indicate the title of a book (e.g., <title> Letter from Birmingham jail </title>) while in another, the <title>...</title> tag may be used to indicate the title of a person (e.g., <title> Dr. </title>). You will learn how to use XML namespaces in Chapter 8.

XML Schema Language: This language is used to define a class of XML documents. As mentioned above, you can use XML to create your own markup language by specifying its vocabulary and grammar. Among the tools available for this language-creation work are XML schemas. You will learn how to use them in Chapter 9.

Extensible Stylesheet Language: XSL is used to define a document's appearance (the fonts and colors it uses, the dimensions along which it displays, etc.), and to transform an XML document from one format to another (e.g., from MARCXML to HTML). XSL will be covered in Chapter 10, with a focus on XML-to-HTML transformation.

XML Path Language: XPath is a language for addressing parts of an XML document. For example, you can use XPath language to locate the first word of the tenth paragraph of an XML document. You will learn some basic XPath language in Chapter 10 in conjunction with our discussion of XSL.

These are just some of the most common XML technologies that you will encounter and use in the library world. XML's flexibility means that there are infinite applications. In this book, we will focus on the technologies that are most common in library settings.

2 XML APPLICATIONS IN LIBRARIES

Over the past few years, XML has rapidly emerged as the standard language for digital information encoding, exchange, and delivery. It has become the universal format for structuring documents and data in almost all areas of information technology. Libraries, whose primary role is to store and to facilitate the access of information and knowledge, can benefit tremendously from this language. XML offers simple and fast solutions to tasks that previously required a tremendous amount of effort. Because of the popularity of XML, almost all library automation system vendors now support XML.

In the library world, XML is currently an agent of revolution. Since the start of the 21st century, library professionals have been discussing the use of XML to replace or supplement almost all kinds of technologies. Here are just some examples.

DIGITAL LIBRARIES

Almost all digital libraries use XML, from preparing electronic documents all the way to online delivery, even recording transaction logs, you will find XML as the primary language of operations. Some famous examples that have been cited in different library literatures include the Networked Digital Library of Theses and Dissertations, the Computing and Information Technology Interactive Digital Educational Library, the National Science Digital Library, and the California Digital Library.

ENCODING TEXT COLLECTIONS

In the area of text encoding and digital-collection building, the most important XML application may be the TEI (Text Encoding Initiative) Standards.

The TEI Standards are an international and interdisciplinary standard that enables libraries, museums, publishers, and individual scholars to adapt literary and linguistic texts for online research, teaching, and preservation. To give you an intuitive understanding of how XML is used here, let's look at an example, which is a header of a possibleTEI document:

```
<teiHeader>
<fileDesc>...</fileDesc>
<encodingDesc>... ...</encodingDesc>
<profileDesc>... ...</profileDesc>
<revisionDesc>... ...</revisionDesc>
</teiHeader>
```

The above example consists of a container (i.e., <teiHeader> ... </teiHeader>), which contains four components inside it, each one of them is also a container, with more information contained. Using the terminology of XML, we called the container a parent element, which has four child elements, where:

- <fileDesc>...</fileDesc> represents the File Description child element, it contains a full bibliographic description of an electronic file;
- <encodingDesc>... ...</encodingDesc> represents the Encoding description child element, it documents the relationship between an electronic text and the source or sources from which it was derived;
- <profileDesc>... ...</profileDesc> represents the Text Profile description child element, it provides a detailed description of non-bibliographic aspects of a text, specifically the languages and sublanguages used, the situation in which it was produced, the participants and their setting; and
- <revisionDesc>... ...</revisionDesc> represents the Revision Description child element, it summarizes the revision history for a file.

TEI was originally sponsored by the Association of Computers in the Humanities (ACH), the Association for Computational Linguistics (ACL), and the Association of Literary and Linguistic Computing (ALLC). There are hundreds of national institutions in the world using TEI for their digital projects. Some high-profile examples include the American Memory (the Library of Congress), the Consortium for Interchange of Museum Information, the Oxford Text Archive, and the Center for Electronic Texts in the Humanities (CETH).

LIBRARY AUTOMATION

In the area of library automation of circulation and other library functions, almost all library system vendors now provide XML support, and many "home-grown" local systems use XML for their system development. Examples include Oregon State Library's interlibrary loan system, State Library of Tasmania's Unified E-government portal, and Washington Research Library Consortium's ALADIN services.

LIBRARY TECHNICAL SERVICES

In the area of technical services, especially in cataloging and classification, new XML DTDs (Document Type Definition) and XML Schemas are proposed and updated almost every year. DTD and Schema are for defining legal document structure. MODS (Metadata Object Description Standard) is one of the most commonly used XML Schemas for bibliographic data in the library world. MODS is developed and maintained by the Library of Congress. The following is part of the schema. It defines a special-purpose XML language with an element named modsCollection, which is to be used to contain a collection of bibliographic records in XML format.

```
<xsd:element name="modsCollection">
   <xsd:complexType>
      <xsd:sequence>
         <xsd:element ref="mods" maxOccurs="unbounded"/>
      </xsd:sequence>
   </xsd:complexType>
</xsd:element>
```

XML Schema is an advanced skill. You can consider the <xsd:complexType>, <xsd:sequence>, etc., as types of commands from the W3C XML Schema language. They are used to define the structure of XML documents that conform to the schema. You will learn how to create and use XML Schema in Chapter 9.

In addition to MODS, there are quite a few important XML Schemas in the area of technical services. For instances, we have MADS (Metadata Authority Description Standard), which is an XML Schema for authority data; we have EAD (Encoded Archival Description), which is an XML markup designed for encoding finding aids for archives; we have MIX (NISO Metadata for Images in XML), which is an XML Schema for encoding technical data elements required to manage digital image collections; and we have PREMIS (Preservation Metadata), which is a data dictionary with supporting XML Schemas for core preservation metadata needed to support the long-term preservation of digital materials. These are only a few, and they are all national standards.

Readers who are interested in reading more about the use of XML in the library can consult Roy Tennant (ed's.) *XML in Libraries*, (Neal-Schuman). In principle, you can use XML to support or facilitate almost all the areas of library functions. In this book, we will focus on using XML to encode metadata, primarily bibliographic data.

11

BASIC XML TECHNIQUES

3 CREATING AND ORGANIZING AN XML DOCUMENT

SAMPLE XML DOCUMENT

What is an XML document? Let's start with a concrete example. Example 3-1 is an XML document. It is your first exercise. Create the document and save it with the filename "ex03A.xml." If you are not using an XML editor program, you can use a word-processing program (e.g., Notepad, MS Word, WordPerfect, etc.) to create the file. Use the "save as" option of your program to save it in plain text file type. Some word processing programs will allow you to choose a particular encoding format when you use the "save as" option to save file in plain text file type. If so, select the UTF-8 format. There will be more discussion about encoding formats and UTF-8 in the following section.

Example 3-1: A simple XML document – filename: "ex03A.xml"

```
<?xml version="1.0" encoding="UTF-8"?>
<record>
    <title>The ugly duckling</title>
    <creator>Hans Christian Andersen</creator>
    <subject>Fairy tales</subject>
    <subject>PZ8.A542</subject>
</record>
```

Example 3-1 is a brief bibliographic description in XML form of Hans Christian Andersen's *The Ugly Duckling*. The line numbers at the left are not part of the document. Indents in the example are for easier reading. Whether you have indents or not is insignificant for the examples in this book. Let's examine this simple XML document.

THE PROLOG AND XML DECLARATION

An XML document consists of two parts: a **prolog** and a **document element** (also called root element). In this section we will discuss the prolog and leave the document element for the next section.

An XML document prolog contains declarations and processing instructions. In Example 3-1, the prolog has only one line (i.e., line 1), which is an **XML declaration**. An XML declaration must open with a left (opening) angle bracket followed by a question mark, followed by the 3 letters xml (i.e., <?xml). The prolog also must end with a question mark and close with a right (closing) angle bracket (?>). The XML declaration informs the processing program that it is an XML document and should be processed accordingly. It also provides some useful parameters for proper processing. In Example 3-1, two parameters are listed in the XML declaration: version="1.0" and encoding="UTF-8."

In addition to the XML declaration, the prolog can contain other declarations (e.g., document type declaration, see Chapter 6) and processing instructions (e.g., style instruction, see Chapters 5 and 10).

Version: There are two versions of XML: 1.0 and 1.1. The W3C's XML 1.0 Recommendation was issued in 1998, and the 1.1 Recommendation was issued in 2004. If a document follows the 1.0 Recommendation, XML declaration is optional. If a document follows the 1.1 Recommendation, it must have the XML declaration as the first line of the document. Many programs that accept XML documents as input can still only accept version 1.0 XML documents. The difference between two versions is not significant for the topics covered in this book. We will use version="1.0" for all our examples.

Encoding: Encoding a document means representing its character data according to a standard such that different computers and programs can process the character data consistently. For example, the English alphabet and punctuation can be represented by different encoding schemes, such as US-ASCII and ISO-8859-1. UTF-8 is a character encoding scheme used to represent Unicode, which is a coding standard for the alphabets of almost every written language in common use on the planet. XML documents use Unicode. There are a few different encoding schemes for Unicode. Most XML documents use UTF-8 as their encoding scheme. We use encoding="UTF-8" for all examples in this book.

ELEMENTS

In an XML document, its basic unit of data is called an element. In Example 3-1, line 2 shows a <record> tag standing all by itself. This is an example of a **start-tag**. On line seven, we see </record>, likewise standing by itself. This is an example of an **end-tag**. Taken together, these two tags look like boundaries of a container housing four items (on lines 3–6); each item is itself defined with an opening and closing tag. In XML terminology, we say there is a **parent element**, record, which contains four **child elements**, that is, one title element, one creator element, and two subject elements. The boundary tags—in this case <record> and </record>—are called **element tags**.

Element tags contain contents inside them, using **start-tags** and **end-tags**. A start-tag consists of the name an element enclosed inside a pair of angle brackets, e.g., <record> is a start-tag of an element whose name is record. An end-tag consists of the same element name as the start-tag, proceeded by a forward slash, and it is also enclosed inside a pair of angle brackets, e.g., </record> is the end-tag of the record element.

In an XML document, after the prolog, there is a **root element** or **document element**, which encloses all other elements and contents of the document. In Example 3-1, the root element is record.

ELEMENT NAME AND XML NAME

You can use almost any combination of characters and numbers to name your element, but there are certain restrictions, particularly regarding spacing and punctuation. The same constraints apply to the names of other XML constructs (e.g., attribute names, etc.) Collectively, we called names that satisfy the constraints **XML names**. Here are the rules:

1. There are only 4 punctuation characters you can use: underscore (_), hyphen (-), period (.), and colon (:). No other punctuation characters are allowed.
2. An XML name must not contain white spaces (e.g., space, tab, line feed, etc.)
3. An XML name must not start with the 3 letters XML (in any combination of uppercase or lowercase).
4. An XML name must not start with a number, hyphen, or period.

An XML name is case sensitive. In other words, Record is not the same as record.

ELEMENT CONTENT

The content of an element can be elements or character data. In Example 3-1, the content of the record element consists of elements, while the contents of the title, creator, and subject elements are character data.

An element can have both elements as well as character data as its content. This kind of content is called "mixed content."

An element also can have no content; this is called "empty element." An empty element can be represented by a start-tag immediately followed by end-tag without any content in between (e.g.: <name></name>), or you can use an empty element tag, which looks like a start-tag, but it has a space and a forward slash before closing with the angle bracket: <name />. Although empty element has no content, it still can convey information. For example, in XHTML, an encoding language written in XML, empty elements <hr /> and <br /> are used to specify horizontal line and line breaks. An empty element also can have attributes that provide additional information about elements. You will learn more about attributes later in the chapter.

Since an element can contain other elements, elements have a hierarchical relationship with each other, like nodes in a family tree. In example 3-1,

1. The record element is the parent of the title, creator, and subject elements.
2. The title, creator, and subject elements are the children of the record element.
3. The title, creator, and subject elements are siblings.

ELEMENT TYPE

You should be aware of the difference between element and element type. Elements of the same name are of the same type, but elements of the same type can have different content. In Example 3-1, there are five elements, but there are only four element types (i.e., record, title, creator, and subject); the subject element appears twice.

COMMENTS

You can add comments to an XML document to leave notes to readers. Comments may appear almost anywhere in an XML document outside other markup (e.g., outside of element tags, processing instructions, etc.) A comment begins with a left angle bracket, followed by an exclamation mark, and then followed by two hyphens (<!--). It ends with two hyphens and a right angle bracket (-->). See Example 3-2, lines 2 and 3. You can have any text or combination of letters, numbers, and symbols in a comment except double hyphens. You cannot use a dash followed immediately by another dash in a comment.

Modify Example 3-1 to match Example 3-2 by adding two comments (line 2 and line 3). Also, add a Collection element (lines 4 and 18) and a record element. Save it with filename: "ex03B.xml." Be careful when you insert comments if you are using a word-processing program. Some word-processing programs will automatically convert double hyphens to a long dash; some will convert a hyphen followed by a left angle bracket to an arrow symbol. If this happens, undo the conversion before saving the file.

Example 3-2: An XML document of two record elements and comments – filename: "ex03B.xml"

```
1  <?xml version="1.0" encoding="UTF-8"?>
2  <!-- draft, not ready for final use yet -->
3  <!-- maybe we can add a <date> element to record when the record was created? -->
4  <Collection>
5  <record >
6      <title>The ugly duckling</title>
7      <creator>Hans Christian Andersen</creator>
8      <subject>Fairy tales</subject>
9      <subject>PZ8.A542</subject>
10 </record>
11 <record>
12     <title>The thief and his master</title>
13     <creator>Jacob Grimm</creator>
14     <creator>Wilhelm Grimm</creator>
15     <subject>Fairy tales</subject>
16     <subject>PZ8.G883</subject>
17 </record>
18 </Collection>
```

In addition to demonstrating the use of comments, Example 3-2 also demonstrates other important features of an XML document. The root element is now Collection, not record; the latter has become a child element of Collection. The purpose of this modification is to demonstrate that you can have as many levels as needed in the hierarchical structure. You can use one record per document, giving you multiple documents for multiple records. You can also create a collection of records in one single XML document by putting multiple record elements in a container element (in this case, the Collection element.) This is called nesting. In an XML document, elements can be nested (i.e., they have parent-children relationships), but they cannot be partially overlapped (i.e., you cannot have part of a record element inside the Collection element and the rest of the record outside the same Collection element).

There are two record elements in Example 3-2. The first record element contains one subject element. The second contains two creator elements. This is to demonstrate that the content of elements of the same element type does not need to have an identical structure. Each can have its own characteristics. You will learn more about how to specify the allowed content of an element in Chapter 6.

ATTRIBUTES

Elements may have associated properties called **attributes**. You use attributes to provide additional information, qualification, or constraint to an element and its content.

For instance, you may want to specify for the subject elements that their contents come from different systems. In Example 3-2, the content of the two subject elements on line 8 and line 15 is the same, i.e., "Fairy tales," which is a Library of Congress Subject Heading (LCSH), while the contents of another two subject elements on line 9 and line 16 are different, i.e., "PZ8.A542" and "PZ8.G883," which are Library of Congress Classification Numbers (LCC). You can add an attribute to each subject element to provide such information, like <subject terms="LCSH"> . . . </subject> and <subject terms="LCC"> . . . </subject>, where terms is the name of the attribute.

You can use almost any combination of characters as an attribute name. The rules about what can be used as an attribute name are the same as the rules for element names (i.e., attribute names must be XML names; see section titled "Element Name and XML Name"). An attribute can only appear inside a start-tag or an empty-element tag. Inside the tag, it follows the name of the element, with the format: *<elementName attributeName="attributeValue">*

The *attributeValue* must be enclosed in single or double quotation marks. It cannot contain an ampersand (&) or left angle bracket (<) Optionally you can use spaces to separate the element name, the attribute name, the attribute value, and the equal sign for the purpose of easy reading. For example, instead of <subject terms="LCSH">Fairy tales</subject>, you can have <subject terms = "LCSH">Fairy tales</subject> (note the space preceeding and following the equal sign.) However, you cannot put spaces between the open angle bracket and the element name, and you cannot use space for padding inside the quotation marks that enclose the attribute value.

Let's create an XML document with attributes. Create Example 3-3, and save it with filename "ex03C.xml." Note that there are three record elements. Each one of them has three attributes: recNum, cataloger, and date. The subject elements also have attributes.

Example 3-3: An XML document with attributes attached to some elements – filename: "ex03C.xml"

```
1  <?xml version="1.0" encoding="UTF-8"?>
2  <!-- draft, not ready for final use yet -->
3  <Collection>
4  <record recNum="FT-0001" cataloger="Kwong Bor Ng" date="2006-10-24">
5      <title>The ugly duckling</title>
6      <creator>Hans Christian Andersen </creator>
7      <subject terms="LCSH">Fairy tales</subject>
8      <subject terms="LCC">PZ8.A542</subject>
9  </record>
10 <record recNum="FT-0002" date="2006-11-16" cataloger="Kwong Bor Ng">
11     <title>The thief and his master</title>
12     <creator>Jacob Grimm</creator>
13     <creator>Wilhelm Grimm</creator>
14     <subject terms="LCSH">Fairy tales</subject>
15     <subject terms="LCC"> PZ8.G883 </subject>
16 </record>
17 <record date="2006-12-21" cataloger="Kwong Bor Ng" recNum="RN-0001">
18     <title>Notes from the Underground</title>
19     <creator> Feodor Dostoevsky</creator>
20     <subject terms="LCSH">Russia -- Officials and employees -- Fiction.</subject>
21     <subject terms="LCC"> PG3326.Z4</subject>
22 </record>
23 </Collection>
```

An element can have more than one attribute. However, unlike element names, attribute names (of the same element) are not repeatable. In other words, when an element has multiple attributes, all of them must be different. The order of the attributes in an element is not significant. The order of the attributes on lines 4, 10, and 17 are all different from each other, and it is perfectly valid.

PROCESSING AN XML DOCUMENT: SPECIAL CHARACTERS, SKIPPING DATA, ENTITIES, AND ENTITY REFERENCES

When a program reads an XML document, its first task is to determine the document's structure and the properties of its data. No processing is begun until these fundamentals are established. If the document contains incorrect tagging or other errors, the processor may warn the user, ask for instructions, or simply stop running. This initial determination is called **parsing**, and in most programs it is undertaken by a module called a parser.

In order to function properly, a parser needs to know what type of data it is being fed. Data in an XML document can take one of two forms: parsed character data (PCDATA) or character data (CDATA). A parser must also know whether there are any entities or entity references in the document. This chapter explains the meaning of PCDATA, CDATA, entities and entity references, and what an XML parser does with them.

PCDATA

If an element contains plain text as its content, we say it contains parsed character data (always called PCDATA in XML documents and applications); this type of data must be parsed before any further processing is undertaken. One of the reasons we parse text is the natural limitations of common input devices. There are many characters that cannot be produced by everyday input devices, such as computer keyboards. To include those characters, we use a code made up of readily available characters and rely on the parsing process to replace those codes with the special characters we intend to display.

For instance, let's say you want to type a copyright sign (©) into an XML document, like this: <right> © ABC Library 2007 </right>. There is no copyright key on a standard computer keyboard. Some word processors allow you to input special signs and symbols using keystroke combinations, but this method tends to be unique to each word-processing program and to be usable only when a document is saved in an extended format, such as

.doc or .rtf. Remember, an XML document must ultimately be saved as plain text, at which point any special, proprietary formatting is lost.

To include a sign or symbol like a copyright sign in an XML document, you can use a numeric-character reference to represent it. As its name suggests, a numeric-character reference uses numbers to represent symbols or signs. There are two standard numeric-character reference systems accepted by XML: decimal and hexadecimal. Decimal references are in the form &#[number]; while hexadecimal references are in the form &#x[number]; (note that there is a letter x, and the number should be a hexadecimal number). For example, a copyright sign can be represented by the decimal character reference © or the hexadecimal character reference ©. You can find a table of common numeric character references in Appendix 4 of this book. Returning to our example, instead of entering <right> © ABC Library 2007 </right>, we would enter <right> © ABC Library 2007 </right> or <right> © ABC Library 2007 </right>. After parsing, the reference will be converted into a copyright sign.

Numeric-character references are also helpful when representing foreign characters. Let's say you want to put the element <author>吴 江 波</author> into an XML document, but you don't have a Chinese character input device. You can use the hexadecimal character references and type in <author> 吳江波 </author>. After parsing, the three hexadecimal character references will be converted to their corresponding Chinese characters, and an XML application will have no problem recognizing and processing them accordingly as parsed character data.

Because it is wiser in this case to err on the side of caution, character data contained in an element will always be parsed unless you provide explicit instructions not to do so. Thus, when an element contains any string of characters as its content, we say that it contains parsed character data. In the previous chapter's examples (Examples 3-1, 3-2, and 3-3), the title, creator, and subject elements all contain parsed character data as their contents.

CDATA

An XML document consists of intermingled character data and markup (tags). One of the tasks performed by an XML parser is to separate character data from markup so that it can check the correctness of the document structure. If you know some parts of the text will be interpreted incorrectly during parsing, you can instruct the parser to skip those parts of the text.

Character data that does not need parsing is called **CDATA**, and the parts of the text that should be skipped by an XML parser are called CDATA sections. CDATA sections may occur anywhere outside markup. They always begin with the nine-character string <![CDATA[(i.e., an open

left angle bracket, an exclamation mark, and an open [left] square bracket, followed by the five letters CDATA, followed by another open [left] square bracket). They always end with the three-character string]]> (two right square brackets followed by a right angle bracket.) Let's build on an earlier example to demonstrate the use of CDATA.

Suppose your library follows the Anglo-American Cataloging Rules in creating catalog records, and you have to add a new record element into the Collection element for a new resource with the following title: *Andersen & his fairy tales*. Since this title is taken from the chief source of information prescribed by the cataloging rules, you should transcribe it to the title field of the record, i.e., <title> Andersen & his fairytales </title>. However, you cannot use the ampersand in the title directly because the ampersand has special meaning in an XML document: all XML entities start with an ampersand. (You will learn about entities in the next section.) When an XML parser sees this ampersand, it will think this is the start of an entity name; but we know that it is just a humble ampersand. There are several solutions to this problem. One of them is to use a CDATA section to instruct the parser not to parse the ambiguous character. Therefore, instead of having <title> Andersen & his fairytales </title>, your record element should be <title> <![CDATA[Andersen & his fairytales]]> </title>. Create Example 4-1 and save it as "ex04A.xml."

Example 4-1: An XML document with a CDATA section – filename: "ex04A.xml"

```
<?xml version="1.0" encoding="UTF-8"?>
<!-- draft, not ready for final use yet -->
<Collection>
<record recNum="FT-0001" cataloger="Kwong Bor Ng" date="2006-10-24">
    <title>The ugly duckling</title>
    <creator>Hans Christian Andersen </creator>
    <subject terms="LCSH">Fairy tales</subject>
    <subject terms="LCC">PZ8.A542</subject>
</record>
<record recNum="FT-0002" date="2006-11-16" cataloger="Kwong Bor Ng">
    <title>The thief and his master</title>
    <creator>Jacob Grimm</creator>
    <creator>Wilhelm Grimm</creator>
    <subject terms="LCSH">Fairy tales</subject>
    <subject terms="LCC"> PZ8.G883 </subject>
</record>
<record date="2006-12-21" cataloger="Kwong Bor Ng" recNum="RN-0001">
```

(cont'd.)

Example 4-1: An XML document with a CDATA section – filename: "ex04A.xml" ***(Continued)***

```
    <title>Notes from the Underground</title>
    <creator>Fyodor Dostoevsky</creator>
    <subject terms="LCSH">Russia -- Officials and employees -- Fiction.</subject>
    <subject terms="LCC">PG3326.Z4</subject>
</record>
<record recNum="FT-0003" cataloger="Kwong Bor Ng" date="2006-12-22">
    <title> <![CDATA[ Andersen & his fairytales ]]> </title>
    <creator>Hans Christian Andersen</creator>
    <subject terms="LCSH">Fairy tales</subject>
    <subject terms="LCC">PZ8.A542</subject>
</record>
</Collection>
```

ENTITIES AND ENTITY REFERENCES

In XML, you can use entities to store information for later retrieval by entity references. Before using an entity reference, you usually need to first declare and define the entity. However, there are **predefined entities** that you can use directly without declaring them. In this section, we will use predefined entities to learn how to use entities and entity references. You will learn how to declare and define your own entities in Chapter 7.

An entity reference has the following format: &[name]; (i.e., an ampersand sign, followed by the name of the entity, followed by a semicolon). For example, lt is a predefined entity that stores just one character, the less-than sign (<), which is the same as the left angle bracket. If you have < in the content of an element, an XML parser will convert it to be a left angle bracket before any other manipulation.

This is crucially important since left angle brackets have a special meaning in XML (they form the start of a markup tag). When an XML parser sees a left angle bracket, it will expect to see a markup tag. Regardless of context, it will treat the characters after the bracket as the name of a tag, which will pretty well guarantee confusion if you use the angle bracket incorrectly. If you intend to use an open angle bracket in the content of an element, you must make allowances for the parser's singlemindedness, or your data will not be processed correctly. You can either use a CDATA section (see Section "CDATA") to instruct the parser to overlook the bracket, or you can use an entity reference (i.e., <). Using either technique to avoid incorrect parsing is called **escaping**. Entity references are commonly used for escaping, and they are often more elegant and efficient to write than using CDATA sections.

As mentioned earlier, the ampersand has special meaning in XML. If you want to use an ampersand literally in the content of an XML element, it needs to be escaped. In this case, the predefined entity reference is &. For instance, in Example 4-1, instead of using a CDATA section, we can use an entity reference (<title>Andersen & his fairytales</title>). Both approaches will cause the element's content to be parsed as <title>Andersen & his fairytales</title>.

Create Example 4-2, and save it with filename "ex04B.xml."

Example 4-2: An XML document with a predefined entity reference – filename: "ex04B.xml"

```
<?xml version="1.0" encoding="UTF-8"?>
<!-- draft, not ready for final use yet -->
<Collection>
<record recNum="FT-0001" cataloger="Kwong Bor Ng" date="2006-10-24">
    <title>The ugly duckling</title>
    <creator>Hans Christian Andersen </creator>
    <subject terms="LCSH">Fairy tales</subject>
    <subject terms="LCC">PZ8.A542</subject>
</record>
<record recNum="FT-0002" date="2006-11-16" cataloger="Kwong Bor Ng">
    <title>The thief and his master</title>
    <creator>Jacob Grimm</creator>
    <creator>Wilhelm Grimm</creator>
    <subject terms="LCSH">Fairy tales</subject>
    <subject terms="LCC"> PZ8.G883 </subject>
</record>
<record date="2006-12-21" cataloger="Kwong Bor Ng" recNum="RN-0001">
    <title> Notes from the Underground </title>
    <creator>Fyodor Dostoevsky</creator>
    <subject terms="LCSH">Russia -- Officials and employees -- Fiction.</subject>
    <subject terms="LCC">PG3326.Z4</subject>
</record>
<record recNum="FT-0003" cataloger="Kwong Bor Ng" date="2006-12-22">
    <title>Andersen &amp; his fairytales</title>
    <creator>Hans Christian Andersen </creator>
    <subject terms="LCSH">Fairy tales</subject>
    <subject terms="LCC">PZ8.A542</subject>
</record>
</Collection>
```

In XML there are three more predefined entities that can be used without declaring. They are: gt (the greater-than sign [>], which is the same as right angle bracket), apos (apostrophe mark, [’]) and quot (quotation mark ["]). Accordingly, the corresponding entity references are >, &apo; and ".

A WELL-FORMED XML DOCUMENT

By now, you have a basic idea of what an XML document looks like and some special considerations that go into forming XML documents properly. The following is a summary with some additional information.

- An XML document consists of a document prolog and a document element (aka root element). The root element contains all the elements in the document.
- The content of an element is delimited by a start-tag and a matching end-tag. A start-tag consists of a pair of angle brackets enclosing the name of the element. An end-tag consists of a pair of angle brackets enclosing the same name with a preceding forward slash.
- For all non-root elements, if the start-tag is in the content of another element, the end-tag must also be in the content of that same element.
- The text of an XML document consists of markup (tags) and character data. There are two characters that cannot appear directly in the character data: the ampersand (&) and the left angle bracket (<). The former is the start delimiter of an entity reference, and the latter is the start delimiter of an element tag. You must escape them using references (& and <).
- An element can have attributes. Attributes are placed in the start-tag or in an empty element tag after the element name, with the attribute values enclosed in quotation marks. The order of the attributes is not important. An attribute name may not be repeated in the same element.
- Comments are not part of character data of an XML document. You can place comments almost anywhere inside an XML document, but they cannot appear inside other markup (i.e., inside start-tags, end-tags, empty-element tags, entity references, processing instructions, etc.)

- Entities can be used for text replacement or to escape ambiguous characters. You use references to retrieve the content of entities. An entity reference is the name of the entity enclosed by two delimiters: an ampersand and a semicolon. There are five predefined entities that you needn't declare prior to use. Besides those five, you can define your own entities; however, they must be declared in the DTD.

If an XML document follows all the above conditions, the document is considered a **well-formed XML document**. Some other rules of thumb pertain to well-formedness, and we will touch on those later in the book.

In principle, an XML document must be well-formed; otherwise it is not an XML document. An XML document can also be **valid** if it meets some more conditions. Validity is related to whether the text follows a particular structure or grammar as defined by a DTD or some other schema language. You will learn how to do that in Parts 3 and 4 of this book.

5 VIEWING XML DOCUMENTS: USING CASCADING STYLE SHEETS (CSS)

VIEWING XML DOCUMENTS WITHOUT STYLE INSTRUCTIONS

Because of their hierarchical structure, XML documents can be described as document trees, much like family trees. In a family tree, there is a point of origin, or "trunk." This trunk splits into branches, sub-branches, and, finally, leaves. Among these levels, there are hierarchical relationships among ancestors, descendants, parents, children, and siblings. When an XML document is represented as a document tree, its elements are the branches. The end nodes (leaves) of an XML document tree can be either text nodes or element nodes.

When a Web browser looks at an XML document, it views it as a document tree. Developers can apply style instructions that cause elements of an XML file to be rendered in more graphically interesting ways, but every XML document is initially seen by Web browsers as a document tree.

Without style instructions, browsers will display the contents of XML files to users in the only way they know how: as document trees. Each Web browser has its own way of rendering document trees. Some will display the XML declaration and part of the document prolog; some will not. Some browsers will display neither the XML declaration nor any information from the prolog, but will display a header message to let the viewer know why a document tree is displayed instead of some formatted content.

For example, try using FireFox or Netscape to view Example 4-2 (filename: "ex04B.xml"). It will look like Figure 5.1.

Notice the minus signs in front of the parent elements in the document tree display. These indicate open elements that can be collapsed. After clicking one of the minus signs, its child elements will be hidden, and it will change to a plus sign (see Figure 5-2). You can click on the plus signs to expand the display back to its original format.

The display is structured, but dry. Aesthetics aside, you may not want to display every last bit of content available to you. For example, the cataloger's name may be useful for internal control, but it is meaningless to general users. You may want to hide it from display, or at least format it in

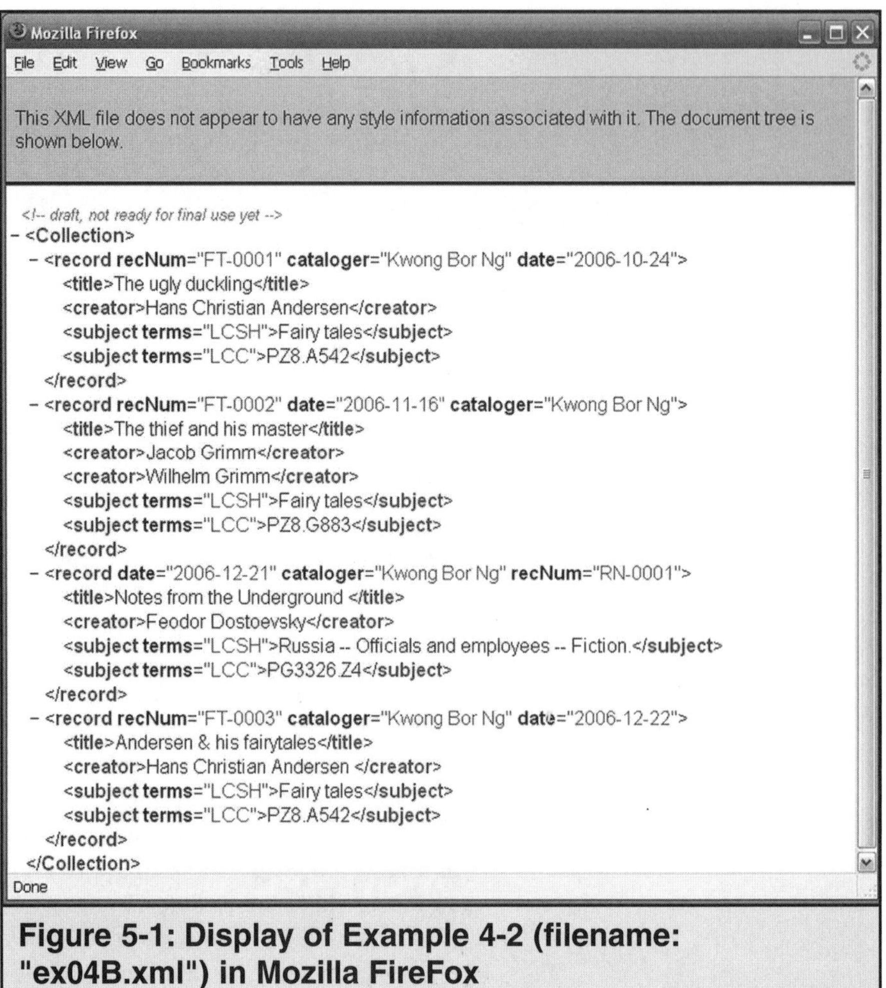

Figure 5-1: Display of Example 4-2 (filename: "ex04B.xml") in Mozilla FireFox

such a way that it does not have the same apparent weight as other, more generally interesting parts of the document. To do this, you will need to use a style sheet.

HOW STYLE SHEETS WORK

What XML documents do for data, style sheets do for the presentation and manipulation of that data: allow for a structured, hierarchical, consistent approach to organizing data for future use. If XML answers the question "What is it?" style sheets answer the question "What does it look like, and what can I do with it?"

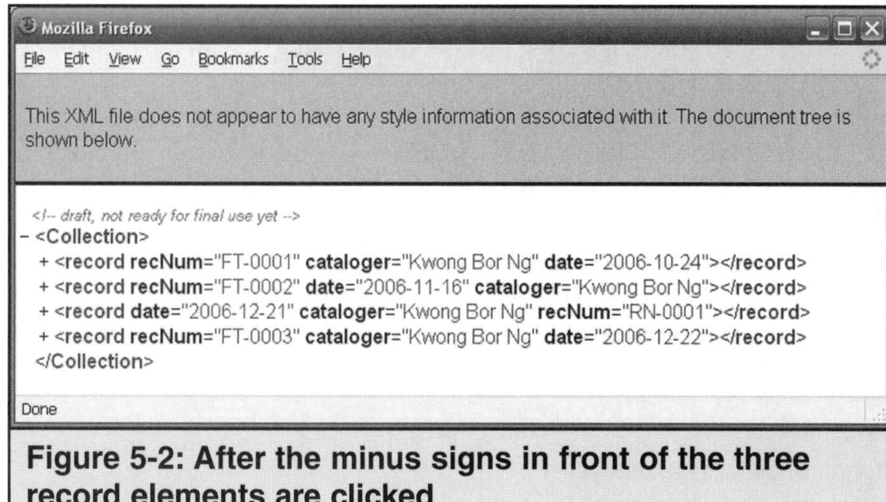

Figure 5-2: After the minus signs in front of the three record elements are clicked

Style sheets allow you to achieve two basic tasks. The first is essentially static and linear, at least when taken alone: modifying the font size and color applied to XML elements; defining the location, size, and color of an element; changing the background image; and so forth. All of these can be achieved using cascading style sheets (CSS).

The second is more dynamic and nonlinear. Using style sheets, you can change the order in which elements are displayed, make computations based on element content, add content to an existing document, combine multiple documents, and more. For these tasks, you need to use a more advanced style language, such as Extensible Style Language (XSL).

Of the two standards, CSS is easier to learn and easier to use. In this chapter, the focus is on CSS; you will learn XSL in Chapter 10.

It will help if you see how style sheets work before delving into a formal discussion of their syntax. Your first exercise of this chapter is to create a very simple CSS file and put it to use. Create Example 5-1 using any text editor, HTML editor, or XML editor. If you use an ordinary text editor, save the file in plain text file type, with filename "ex05A.css."

Example 5-1 is simple and, with a little bit of scrutiny, intuitively understandable. You will learn about the file syntax in the next section; for now, let's start with some observations. There are four lines. Each line begins with

Example 5-1: A very simple CSS file – filename: "ex05A.css"

```
Collection {display: block;}
record {display: block;    margin: 24px;}
title, creator, subject {display: block;}
title {font-weight: bold;}
```

an XML element name (or names), followed by a pair of curly braces. Inside the curly braces are style instructions associated with the element(s). Each instruction consists of two components—a style property and a style value—separated by a colon. Each instruction ends with a semicolon.

To apply this CSS file, add a line of processing instruction to the prolog of "ex04B.xml" (Example 4-2), and save it as "ex05B.xml" (see Example 5-2 line 2.). It should be saved in the same folder as "ex05A.css" (Example 5-1).

Example 5-2: An XML Document associated with a style sheet – filename: "ex05B.xml"

```
1   <?xml version="1.0" encoding="UTF-8"?>
2   <?xml-stylesheet type="text/css" href="ex05A.css"?>
3   <!-- draft, not ready for final use yet -->
4   <Collection>
5   <record recNum="FT-0001" cataloger="Kwong Bor Ng" date="2006-10-24">
6       <title>The ugly duckling</title>
7       <creator>Hans Christian Andersen </creator>
8       <subject terms="LCSH">Fairy tales</subject>
9       <subject terms="LCC">PZ8.A542</subject>
10  </record>
11  <record recNum="FT-0002" date="2006-11-16" cataloger="Kwong Bor Ng">
12      <title>The thief and his master</title>
13      <creator>Jacob Grimm</creator>
14      <creator>Wilhelm Grimm</creator>
15      <subject terms="LCSH">Fairy tales</subject>
16      <subject terms="LCC"> PZ8.G883 </subject>
17  </record>
18  <record date="2006-12-21" cataloger="Kwong Bor Ng" recNum="RN-0001">
19      <title> Notes from the Underground </title>
20      <creator>Fyodor Dostoevsky</creator>
21      <subject terms="LCSH">Russia -- Officials and employees -- Fiction.</subject>
22      <subject terms="LCC">PG3326.Z4</subject>
23  </record>
24  <record recNum="FT-0003" cataloger="Kwong Bor Ng" date="2006-12-22">
25      <title>Andersen &amp; his fairytales</title>
26      <creator>Hans Christian Andersen </creator>
27      <subject terms="LCSH">Fairy tales</subject>
28      <subject terms="LCC">PZ8.A542</subject>
29  </record>
30  </Collection>
```

The XML document now knows to look to our CSS file for instructions on how to format and display its data. In essence, CSS transforms semantic, non-presentational markup—an XML file built to organize and store data, however drily—into the **presentational markup** that forms a standard Web page. For example, the title element tag is a semantic markup, not a presentational markup. Just by looking at the tag you can tell something about its content, but there is no hint as to how the content should be displayed. On lines 3 and 4 of the CSS file (Example 5-2), the title element is transformed into presentational markup: the content of the element should be displayed in block (i.e., on its own line) and in bold face. Now, if you use a Web browser to view the file "ex05B.xml," it will look like Figure 5-3.

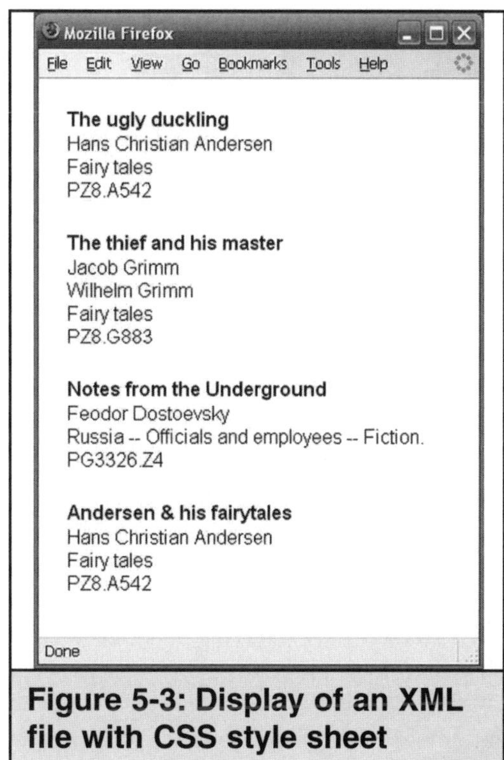

Figure 5-3: Display of an XML file with CSS style sheet

CASCADING STYLE SHEET SYNTAX

CSS is a language that allows authors to attach style information to structured documents like XML and HTML documents. The official W3C recommendation of CSS version 2 was issued in 1998 (see "css2.pdf" under the appendix folder in the accompanying CD), but there are still many features that various Web browsers do not implement. The basic syntax of CSS has not changed since the first version.

To illustrate the syntax of CSS, we need a more complicated document than Example 5-2. Retrieve the file “LittleMatchSeller.txt” from the accompanying CD. Add metadata and encode the document in XML so it looks just like Example 5-3; then save it with the filename “ex05C.xml.” Note that decimal character references are used for the left and right double quotation marks (“ and ”, respectively).

Example 5-3: Andersen's *The Little Match-Seller* – Filename: "ex5C.xml"

```
<?xml version="1.0" encoding="UTF-8"?>
<fairytale>
<metadata >
  <encoder branch="ABC Library New York City Branch">
    <firstname>Kwong</firstname>
    <middlename>Bor</middlename>
    <lastname>Ng</lastname>
  </encoder>
  <descriptive>
    <title>The Little Match-Seller</title>
    <author>
      <firstname>Hans</firstname>
      <middlename>Christian</middlename>
      <lastname>Andersen</lastname>
    </author>
    <year>1846</year>
    <translator>
      <firstname>H.</firstname>
      <middlename>P.</middlename>
      <lastname>Paull</lastname>
    </translator>
  </descriptive>
  <subject>
    <LCC>PZ8.A542</LCC>
    <LCSH>Fairy tales</LCSH>
  </subject>
</metadata>
<maintext>
```

(cont'd.)

Example 5-3: Andersen's *The Little Match-Seller* – Filename: "ex5C.xml" ***(Continued)***

<paragraph>It was terribly cold and nearly dark on the last evening of the old year, and the snow was falling fast. In the cold and the darkness, a poor little girl, with bare head and naked feet, roamed through the streets. It is true she had on a pair of slippers when she left home, but they were not of much use. They were very large, so large, indeed, that they had belonged to her mother, and the poor little creature had lost them in running across the street to avoid two carriages that were rolling along at a terrible rate. One of the slippers she could not find, and a boy seized upon the other and ran away with it, saying that he could use it as a cradle, when he had children of his own. So the little girl went on with her little naked feet, which were quite red and blue with the cold. In an old apron she carried a number of matches, and had a bundle of them in her hands. No one had bought anything from her the whole day, nor had anyone given her even a penny. Shivering with cold and hunger, she crept along; poor little child, she looked the picture of misery. The snowflakes fell on her long, fair hair, which hung in curls on her shoulders, but she regarded them not. </paragraph>

<paragraph>Lights were shining from every window, and there was a savory smell of roast goose, for it was New-year's eve-yes, she remembered that. In a corner, between two houses, one of which projected beyond the other, she sank down and huddled herself together. She had drawn her little feet under her, but she could not keep off the cold; and she dared not go home, for she had sold no matches, and could not take home even a penny of money. Her father would certainly beat her; besides, it was almost as cold at home as here, for they had only the roof to cover them, through which the wind howled, although the largest holes had been stopped up with straw and rags. Her little hands were almost frozen with the cold. Ah! Perhaps a burning match might be some good, if she could draw it from the bundle and strike it against the wall, just to warm her fingers. She drew one out — “scratch!” how it sputtered as it burnt! It gave a warm, bright light, like a little candle, as she held her hand over it. It was really a wonderful light. It seemed to the little girl that she was sitting by a large iron stove, with polished brass feet and a brass ornament. How the fire burned! It seemed so beautifully warm that the child stretched out her feet as if to warm them, when the flame of the match went out, the stove vanished, and she had only the remains of the half-burnt match in her hand. </paragraph>

<paragraph>She rubbed another match on the wall. It burst into a flame, and where its light fell upon the wall it became as transparent as a veil, and she could see into the room. The table was covered with a snowy white table-cloth, on which stood a splendid dinner service, and a steaming roast goose, stuffed with apples and dried plums. And what was still more wonderful, the goose jumped down from the dish and waddled across the floor, with a knife and fork in its breast, to the little girl. Then

(cont'd.)

Example 5-3: Andersen's *The Little Match-Seller* – Filename: "ex5C.xml" *(Continued)*

```
the match went out, and there remained nothing but the thick, damp, cold
wall before her. </paragraph>
<paragraph>She lighted another match, and then she found herself sitting
under a beautiful Christmas-tree. It was larger and more beautifully
decorated than the one which she had seen through the glass door at the
rich merchant's. Thousands of tapers were burning upon the green
branches, and colored pictures, like those she had seen in the show-
windows, looked down upon it all. The little one stretched out her hand
towards them, and the match went out. </paragraph>
<paragraph>The Christmas lights rose higher and higher, till they looked
to her like the stars in the sky. Then she saw a star fall, leaving behind it
a bright streak of fire. <speech>&#8220;Someone is dying,&#8221;
</speech> thought the little girl, for her old grandmother, the only one
who had ever loved her, and who was now dead, had told her that when
a star falls, a soul was going up to God. </paragraph>
<paragraph>She again rubbed a match on the wall, and the light shone
round her; in the brightness stood her old grandmother, clear and shining,
yet mild and loving in her appearance. <speech>&#8220;Grandmother,
&#8221;</speech> cried the little one, <speech>&#8220;O take me with
you; I know you will go away when the match burns out; you will vanish
like the warm stove, the roast goose, and the large, glorious Christmas-
tree.&#8221;</speech> And she made haste to light the whole bundle of
matches, for she wished to keep her grandmother there. And the matches
glowed with a light that was brighter than the noon-day, and her
grandmother had never appeared so large or so beautiful. She took the
little girl in her arms, and they both flew upwards in brightness and joy far
above the earth, where there was neither cold nor hunger nor pain, for
they were with God. </paragraph>
<paragraph>In the dawn of morning there lay the poor little one, with pale
cheeks and smiling mouth, leaning against the wall; she had been frozen
to death on the last evening of the year; and the New-year's sun rose and
shone upon a little corpse! The child still sat, in the stiffness of death,
holding the matches in her hand, one bundle of which was burnt.
<speech>&#8220;She tried to warm herself,&#8221;</speech> said
some. No one imagined what beautiful things she had seen, nor into what
glory she had entered with her grandmother, on New-year's day.
</paragraph>
</maintext>
</fairytale>
```

Example 5-4 is a simple CSS file, with only two sets of rules. You will add more style instructions along the way. Create Example 5-4, save the file with filename “ex05D.css.”

Example 5-4: A very simple CSS file – filename: "ex05D.css"

```
1   fairytale {
2       display: block;
3       padding: 36px;
4       font-size: 12pt;
5       font-family: Georgia, "Times New Roman";
6       color: darkblue;
7       text-align: justify;
8       background-color: lightblue;
9   }
10  title {
11      display: block;
12      padding: 24px;
13      font-size: 28pt;
14      font-variant: small-caps;
15      text-align: center;
16  }
```

CSS works by mapping elements to sets of style properties. Each mapping is called a rule. There are two rules in Example 5-4. One is for fairytale, the other for title.

A CSS rule takes the form: *selector {property: value; property: value; . . . . . . }* There are two basic components here: (1) A **selector**, which matches an element type, and (2) a **declaration block**, which consists of a list of declarations. Each declaration is a pairing of a style **property** with a style **value**, separated by a colon and ending with a semicolon (i.e., *property: value;*). For easy reading, you can put one property-value pair per line, but you can also put them all together on the same line. The list of the declarations is enclosed by a pair of curly braces.

EXPLANATION OF THE FIRST RULE

The selector of the first rule is fairytale. The list of property-value pairs is just a series of presentational instructions about the font, alignment, and background color to be used (Example 5-4, lines 2–9). Based on the first rule, when "ex05A.css" is associated with an xml file that has fairytale element(s) in it, the content of the fairytale element(s) should be displayed according to the following specifications:

display: block; All elements have a display property. There are many possible values for this property, but the most commonly used are block, inline, and none. When the value is block, the content of the selector element will be displayed on its own line: it will be rendered as if a line break were placed before as well as after the content of the selector element.

padding: 36px; The padding property specifies the width of the padding area. When there is only one value specified, it applies to all the four sides (top, bottom, left, and right) of the area, so there should be 36 pixels on the top, bottom, left, and right of the box occupied by the content of the selector element (i.e., the content of the fairytale element).

font-size: 12pt; You can specify the value of the font-size property using absolute keywords, relative keywords, or specific unit measurements. Keywords of absolute size are xx-small, x-small, small, medium, large, x-large, and xx-large. They are absolute because they refer to the static settings in each user's browser. Keywords of relative size are larger and smaller. These are relative to the values of the font-size property of the parent element. In Example 5-4, a specific unit measurement is used to indicate the size of the font. There are many units you can use in specifying length: px (pixels), pt (points), and so forth. The unit of measurement used here is point. Accordingly, the content (parsed character data) of the fairytale element will be displayed using a 12-point font size.

font-family: Georgia, "Times New Roman"; This means, if the browser has the font Georgia, display the text content (parsed character data) of the selector element (i.e., the fairytale element) in Georgia; otherwise, use Times New Roman. When the name of the font-family property has more than one word, you should use quotation marks to enclose the name, for example, "Times New Roman".

text-align: justify; This property sets the alignment of the textual content (parsed character data) of the selector element. You can use keywords like left, right, center, and justify as values.

color: darkblue; background-color: lightblue; These two properties describe the foreground color and background color of the selector element's text content. To specify a color, you can use a color keyword. In the CSS 2 Recommendation, there are 16 keywords for color: aqua, black, blue, fuchsia, gray, green, lime, maroon, navy, olive, purple, red, silver, teal, white, and yellow. In addition, all Web browsers understand 216 Web-safe colors. Example 5-4 uses darkblue as the foreground color (color of the text) and lightblue as the background color; both are among the 216 Web-safe colors.

If you are familiar with the RGB system instead of a color keyword, you can also use a numerical RGB specification. RGB is a color model accepted by almost all color-rendering computer programs. It represents the percentages (from 0% to 100%) or strength (from 0 to 255) of the three primary colors (red, blue, and green) needed to composite the final color. For example, instead of color: red, you can use: color: rgb(100%, 0%, 0%), which means 100% of red plus 0% of green plus 0% of blue; or color: rgb(255, 0, 0), which means maximum red plus no green and no blue.

EXPLANATION OF THE SECOND RULE

The selector of the second rule is title, and its list of property-value pairs runs from line 11 to line 15. The only new property here is font-variant. Its value can be either small-caps or normal. Based on this rule, the content of title element should be displayed as a block with 24 pixels of padding space; it should be placed at the center of the browser window. The font size should be 28 points. All letters except the first letter of each word should be in smaller uppercase.

There are many more other style properties you can set in CSS. For a complete list, see the file "CSS2.pdf" in the accompanying CD under the Appendices folder.

STYLE INSTRUCTION AS PROCESSING INSTRUCTION

An XML document prolog can contain declaration and processing instruction (PI). Processing instruction is used for sending messages to an application. It must begin with <?*target* and end with ?> where *target* is the name used to identify the application to which the instruction is directed. To add style instruction to an XML file, you can use processing instruction with xml-stylesheet as the target. Usually it takes the follow form: <?xml-stylesheet type="text/css" href=*"locationOfCSSFile"*?>.

If the CSS file is located in the same place as the referencing XML file (i.e., both files are in the same folder of the same computer), you only need to give the filename of the CSS file as the value of the href parameter (e.g., href=*"filenameOfCSSFile"*).

You can also use the Web address of the CSS file as the value of the href parameter. Suppose the CSS file is accessible using the following URL: http://www.justanexample.net/abc.css. Then the processing instruction will be <?xml-stylesheet type="text/css" href="http://www.justanexample.net/abc.css"?>. Note that you can use tab or line break instead of space in the processing instruction for easy reading.

Open "ex05C.xml" (Example 5-3). Insert the following processing instruction <?xml-stylesheet type="text/css" href="ex05D.css"?> between the first line and the second line (i.e., between the XML declaration and the root element fairytale). Save the file with the filename "ex05E.xml." Save it in the same folder as you saved the file "ex05C.css." The first few lines of your file should look like this:

```
<?xml version="1.0" encoding="UTF-8"?>
<?xml-stylesheet type="text/css" href="ex05D.css"?>
<fairytale>
<metadata >
```

Now, if you view the file "ex05E.xml," the display will look like Figure 5-4.

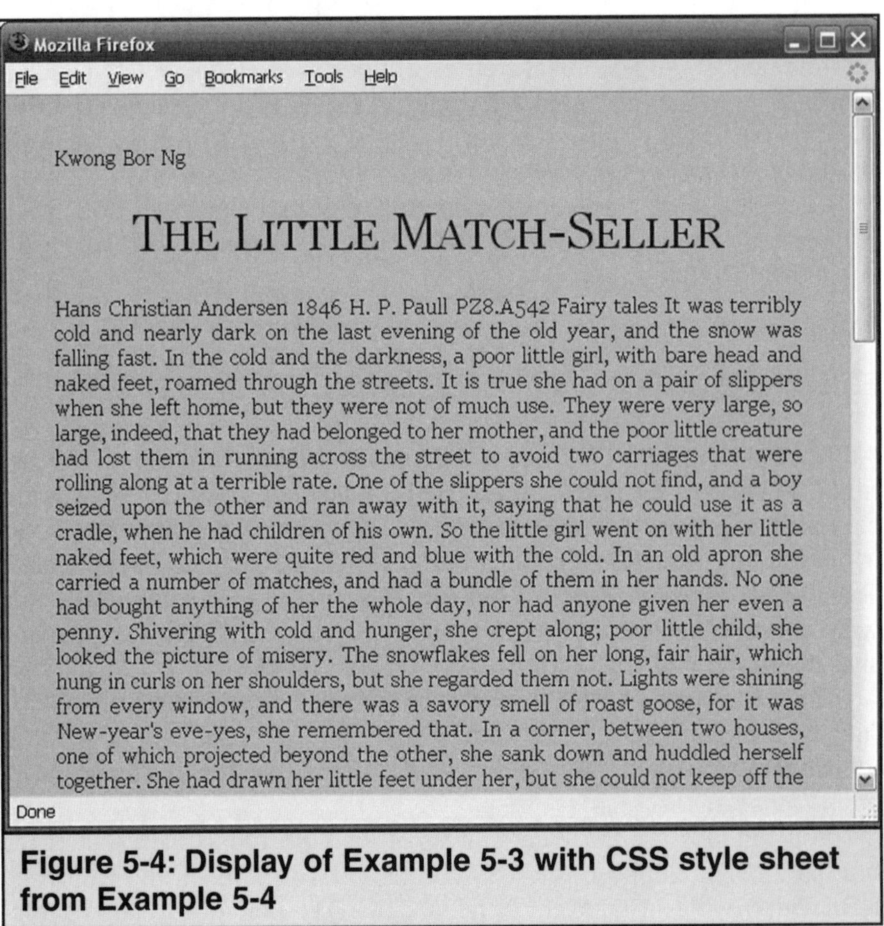

Figure 5-4: Display of Example 5-3 with CSS style sheet from Example 5-4

EXPLANATIONS OF THE DISPLAY

For the first rule in the CSS file (Example 5-4, line 2 to line 9), the selector is fairytale (line 1), which is the root element. Therefore, its property settings apply to the whole document. The descendant elements of fairytale will inherit these property settings unless there are other overriding CSS rules or unless the properties have their own initial (default) values. Hence, in Figure 5-4, there are 36 pixels of padding space surrounding the whole document, the text color should be dark blue, and background color should be light blue.

There are three blocks of text in the display. The first block is the encoder's name. The second block is the title of the fairytale. The third block consists of the remaining content of the document, including metadata. Now, let's examine them one by one.

The first block of text is the content of firstname, middlename, and lastname. In the CSS file (Example 5-4), there is no rule for these three elements. Not all properties of all elements have to be specified explicitly in CSS. If there is no value set for an applicable property of an element, a browser will apply the initial value (i.e., default value) of the property. If an applicable property for an element has no initial value, then it will inherit the value from its parent. For the display property, the initial value is inline. In other words, if an element has no display property specified in the CSS rule, the following rule will be applied: element {display: inline;}. The value inline means: do not start a new line when displaying the content of this element. Therefore, if there is no explicit rule for the display property of an element, the content of the element will be displayed on the same line as the content of its previous element. That is why the contents of firstname, middlename, and lastname are all on the same line.

There are no default values for the font-size, font-family, color, and text-align properties. If there is no instruction about these properties for an element, the initial values will be inherited from its parent element. The parent of the firstname, middlename, and lastname is encoder, and the parent of encoder is metadata. Neither has explicit property settings for the properties. The parent of metadata is fairytale, so the content of firstname, middlename, and lastname are displayed based on the font-size, font-family, color, and text-align properties specified for fairytale.

The second block of text is the content of title. In the CSS file (Example 5-4), there is a rule for title. The content of title is handled exactly as specified by the rule, i.e., 28 points in font size, center alignment on its own line, small uppercase letters for all letters except the first letter of each word, and 24 pixels of padding from all 4 edges. Note that in the rule there is no specification for the font-family property, so that is inherited from fairytale.

The third block of the text consists of all the rest of the document. This is collapsed into one single block because the default value for the display property of no-rule elements is inline. The font-size, font-family, color, etc., is inherited from the fairytale element.

MORE CSS RULES

Suppose you want to make the following changes:

1. Hide the content of encoder, translator; and subject;
2. Show the content of author and year differently;
3. Separate the paragraphs;
4. Display speeches in different color.

Let's add more rules to "ex05D.css" to achieve these goals.

The first rule to add is encoder, translator, subject {display: none;}

In this rule, there are three selectors: encoder, translator, and subject. You can put multiple selectors (separated by comma) in one single CSS rule if they share the same property-value pairs. When the value of the display property is set to none, the content of the selector element will not be shown, including all its descendant elements (i.e., child elements, grandchild elements, etc.). This behavior cannot be overridden by setting the display property on the descendants.

To display the content of author and year differently from the rest of the text, there have to be rules to override the style properties they have inherited from fairytale. Add the following two rules:

1. author {display: block; font-weight: bold; text-align: center; } ,
2. year {display: block; font-style: italic; text-align: center; padding: 12px;},

The former rule will center the content of author in its own block and use boldface font for display. The latter rule will display the content of year in its own block, in italics, with 12 pixels of padding.

To display the content of the paragraph elements in its own block with 12 pixels of padding, add the rule: paragraph {display: block; padding: 12px;}.

To display the content of the speech element in a different color, add the following rule: speech {color: purple;}.

Save the CSS file with the filename "ex05F.css," which should look like Example 5-5.

Example 5-5: A CSS file with more rules – filename: "ex05F.css"

```
fairytale {
    display: block; padding: 36px; font-size: 12pt;
    font-family: Georgia, "Times New Roman"; color: darkblue;
    text-align: justify; background-color: lightblue;
}
title {
    display: block; font-size: 28pt; font-variant: small-caps;
    text-align: center; padding: 24px;
}
encoder, translator, subject {display: none;}
author {display: block; font-weight: bold; text-align: center; }
year {display: block; font-style: italic; text-align: center; padding: 12px;}
paragraph {display: block; padding: 12px;}
speech {color: purple;}
```

Note that you only put in the property-value pairs that you want to specify. All of the non-listed properties will have the initial values, which may be inherited from the parents of the elements. Also note that line break and indent are not significant in the CSS file.

Edit "ex05E.xml" by changing the name of the processing instruction from <?xml-stylesheet type="text/css" href="ex05D.css"?> to <?xml-stylesheet type="text/css" href="ex05F.css"?>. Save the file with the filename "ex05G.xml," in the same folder as you saved the file "ex05F.css."

Now, if you view the file "ex05G.xml" with a browser, it should look like Figure 5.5.

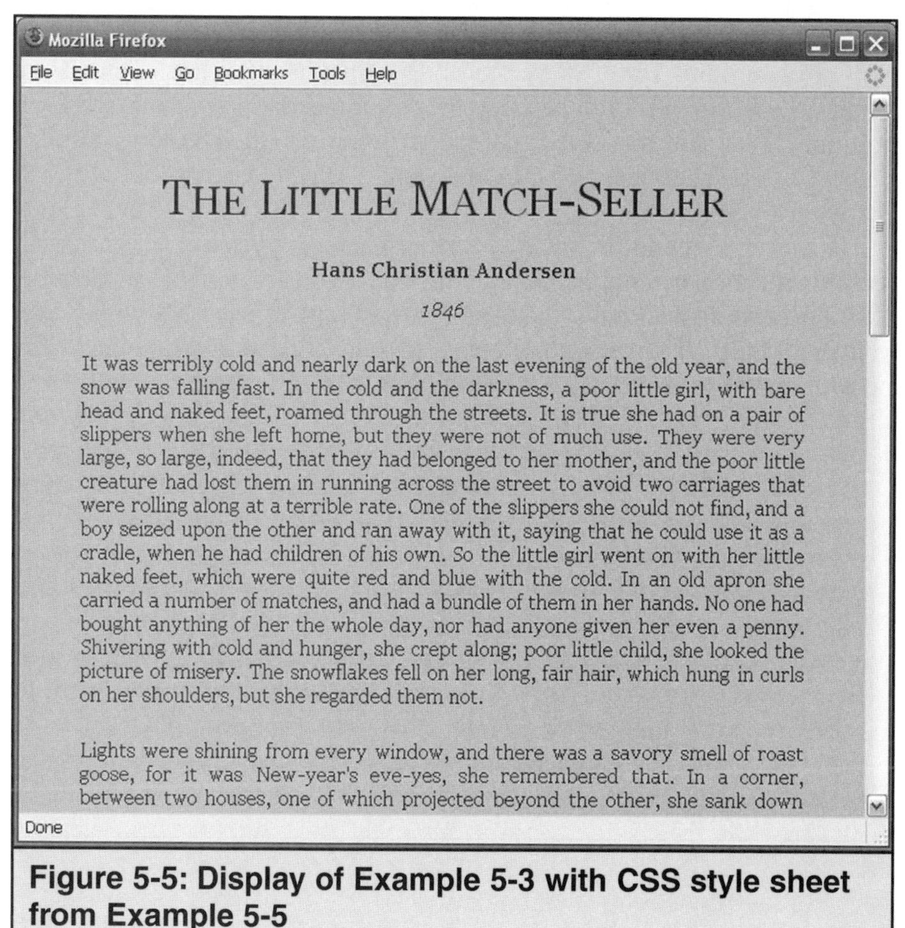

Figure 5-5: Display of Example 5-3 with CSS style sheet from Example 5-5

CAVEAT ON USING THE OFFICIAL CSS2 RECOMMENDATION

Don't be fooled by thinking that because XSL is much more advanced and flexible than CSS, that maybe you should learn XSL instead of CSS. CSS is not just handy and easy to learn, it is also a powerful language. In most cases, CSS is enough for all practical purposes. This chapter barely touches the surfaces of many features of CSS. After you have finished reading this chapter, you should read the Official CSS 2 Recommendation. Just like XML and HTML, CSS is also a standard under the auspices of the W3C Consortium. The CSS version 2 Recommendation has a tutorial on using CSS with XML. You can find the recommendation in the W3C Consortium's Web site for technical reports (www.w3.org/TR). It is also included in the accompanying CD under the "Appendices" folder with the file name "CSS2.pdf."

However, at the time the CSS2 recommendation was written, the XML recommendation had not yet been finalized. If you are going to consult the CSS 2 Recommendation to learn more about how to use CSS with XML, you should also read the article "How to Add Style to XML," which can be accessed at www.w3.org/Style/styling-XML.

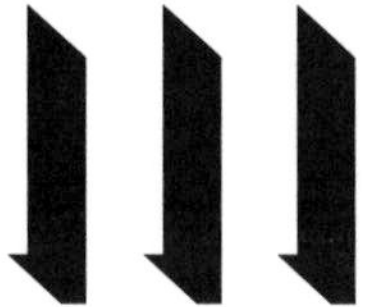

INTERMEDIATE XML TECHNIQUES

ASSIGNING STRUCTURE USING DOCUMENT TYPE DECLARATIONS AND DOCUMENT TYPE DEFINITIONS

A document type declaration (DOCTYPE) identifies the grammar for a class of XML documents. This grammar is called a document type definition (DTD). Its primary job is to specify a logical structure for a conforming XML document. A conforming XML document can only use the vocabularies in the DTD. For example, you can specify the names, attributes, content types, hierarchical relationships, sequential order, and occurrence frequencies for the elements you want in a DTD. An XML document that conforms to this DTD can only use these predefined elements in its content.

Using a DTD, you can ensure that an XML document will have a well-defined structure specifically designed for a particular purpose. In other words, you can create your own special-purpose markup language by creating a DTD. Many markup languages were created using DTDs, including the most commonly used markup language in the world, HTML.

In this chapter, you will learn the basic syntax governing DTDs. You will also create two DTD files, one for a collection of bibliographic records, the other for a narrative text (a fairytale) with simple metadata.

DOCUMENT TYPE DECLARATIONS

As we have seen, the first declaration in the prolog of an XML document should be an XML declaration, such as <?xml version="1.0" encoding="UTF-8"?>. Along with the XML declaration, a prolog can have another declaration: the document type declaration. XML documents that rely on DTDs use document type declarations (DOCTYPE) to associate themselves with the proper DTD.

A document type declaration starts with an open angle (left) bracket and an exclamation mark, followed by the word DOCTYPE: <!DOCTYPE. It ends with a closed (right) angle bracket: <!DOCTYPE … … >. Inside

<!DOCTYPE and > there are two components. The first component identifies the root element. The second component contains or points to a DTD.

A document type declaration can take several formats, depending on whether the DTD is internal, external, or mixed. We will examine each one of them in the following sections.

INTERNAL DTDS

A document type declaration may take the following form: <!DOCTYPE *root-element* [rules]> where *root-element* marks the name of the root element, and *rules* indicates a set of rules specifying the document's grammar (including all allowed vocabularies). This approach is called an internal DTD because the rules are listed inside the XML document.

Let's illustrate this with a simple exercise. Create Example 6-1, and save it with the filename "ex06A.xml." In Example 6-1, lines 2–8 form the document type declaration, which identifies Collection as the root element; lines 3–8 form the DTD. Note the open square bracket at the end of line 2 and the closed square bracket at the beginning of line 8. An internal DTD must be enclosed by square brackets.

Example 6-1: An XML document with an internal DTD – filename: "ex06A.xml"

```
1   <?xml version="1.0" encoding="UTF-8"?>
2   <!DOCTYPE Collection [
3       <!ELEMENT Collection (record)*>
4       <!ELEMENT record  (title | creator | subject)*>
5       <!ELEMENT title (#PCDATA)>
6       <!ELEMENT creator (#PCDATA)>
7       <!ELEMENT subject (#PCDATA)>
8   ]>
9   <?xml-stylesheet type="text/css" href="ex05A.css"?>
10  <Collection>
11  <record >
12      <title>The ugly duckling</title>
13      <creator>Hans Christian Andersen</creator>
14      <subject>Fairy tales</subject>
```

(cont'd.)

Example 6-1: An XML document with an internal DTD – filename: "ex06A.xml" ***(Continued)***

```
15        <subject>PZ8.A542</subject>
16    </record>
17    <record>
18        <title>The thief and his master</title>
19        <creator>Jacob Grimm</creator>
20        <creator>Wilhelm Grimm</creator>
21        <subject>Fairy tales</subject>
22        <subject>PZ8.G883</subject>
23    </record>
24    </Collection>
```

Example 6-1 uses the CSS file from the last Chapter (Example 5-1, filename: “ex05A.css”). If you don’t have the CSS file in the same folder as “ex06A.xml,” you will only see a long line of text when you view Example 6-1 in a Web browser.

In Example 6-1, the rules in the DTD (lines 3–7) are **element type declarations**. You use element type declarations to create new element types and to specify the kind of content that is allowed for each type of element. As mentioned in Chapter 3, you should be aware of the difference between elements and element types. Elements of the same name are of the same type, but elements of the same type can have different contents. In a DTD, you create element types and specify content types, but you do not actually create elements and their contents. You use the element type declared in the DTD to create elements and their contents in the body of an XML document.

An element type declaration takes the form <!ELEMENT *name content-specification*> where <!ELEMENT is the starting delimiter of the declaration, *name* is the name of the element type you want to create, *content-specification* specifies the allowed content of this element type, and > is the end delimiter of the declaration.

There are four possible content specifications: EMPTY, children, mixed, and ANY. An element with no content is said to be empty. In a DTD, you declare an empty element with the following declaration: <!ELEMENT Name EMPTY>. The reserved keyword ANY is used in an element declaration to declare an element that has no specific content constraint. This declaration takes the following form: <!ELEMENT Name ANY>. In Example 6-1, there are no EMPTY or ANY element declarations. The elements in Example 6-1 either have children content (that is, they contain child elements) or mixed content (they contain character data, optionally interspersed with child elements).

In Example 6-1, there are five rules (element type declarations) in the DTD.

(1) <!ELEMENT Collection (record)*>

Here, we declare (or create) an element type called Collection and specify that the content of Collection can consist only of zero or more record elements.

The asterisk in the declaration is a quantity indicator indicating an occurrence constraint; specifically, it means "zero or more occurrences." In other words, inside a Collection element, there can be any number of record elements, or no elements at all, but there cannot be any elements or characters that are not record elements.

In addition to the asterisk, two other symbols are used to specify occurrence constraints: the plus sign and the question mark. The plus sign represents one or more occurrences; the question mark represents zero or one occurrence. For example, if the element type declaration is <!ELEMENT Collection (record)+>, then you must have **at least** one record inside Collection; if it is <!ELEMENT Collection (record)?>, then you must have **at most** one record inside Collection; if it is simply <!ELEMENT Collection (record)>, without any occurrence constraints, then you must have ***exactly*** one record inside Collection. Note that the parentheses in the element type declaration are used strictly for easy grouping. Therefore, when the quantity indicator is used to qualify only one child element, it can be inside or outside the parentheses: (record)? is the same as (record?), and (record+) is the same as (record)+.

(2) <!ELEMENT record (title | creator | subject)*>

In this line, we declare an element type called record and specify that the content of record can only be title or creator or subject or any combination thereof, in any order, with no limitation on the number of occurrences (note the asterisk).

When a parent element contains two or more child element types, the children can be organized and controlled by logical connectors. There are two logical connectors: the choice connector (represented by a vertical pipe: |) and the sequence connector (represented by a comma). In the content-specification part of an element type declaration, when the elements are connected by choice connectors, any one of the elements is allowed as content. If the sequence connector is used, the elements must appear as an ordered sequence. For instance, if the element declaration is <!ELEMENT record (title, creator, subject)*>, a conforming document's record element may only contain sequence(s) of title, creator, and subject. It can have 0 or more occurrences of this sequence. Each sequence must consist of exactly one title element, followed by one creator element, followed by one subject element.

(3) <!ELEMENT title (#PCDATA)>

This line declares an element type called title and specifies that the content of title can only be parsed character data (#PCDATA). Child elements are not allowed inside the title element.

(4–5) <!ELEMENT creator (#PCDATA)> and <!ELEMENT subject (#PCDATA)>

These declarations are essentially identical to <!ELEMENT title (#PCDATA)>; only the element types are different.

In the content part of Example 6-1 (lines 10–24), the root element, Collection, contains two record elements. Each record element has several child elements. Note that the two record elements do not need to have identical composition in order to satisfy the conditions listed in the DTD: the structure of each element follows the grammar specified in the DTD exactly. If you put any element into the document that is not declared in the DTD, or if you do not follow the content specification in the DTD, the XML processor that uses the document as input will complain and stop the processing. Most Web browsers do not contain validating XML parsers: they will parse but will not verify XML documents with DTDs or schemas.

EXTERNAL DTDS

A DTD can be a file unto itself, outside the XML files that depend on it, in which case it is called an external DTD. In this scenario, an XML document contains a reference to the name and location of the DTD on which it depends. This makes it much easier to create and maintain many XML documents, each of which relies on the same DTD. Example 6-2 demonstrates a simple external DTD file. Create it and save it with the filename "ex06B.dtd."

Example 6-2: An external DTD file – filename: "ex06B.dtd"

```
<?xml version="1.0" encoding="UTF-8"?>
<!ELEMENT Collection (record)*>
<!ELEMENT record (title | creator | subject)*>
<!ELEMENT title (#PCDATA)>
<!ELEMENT creator (#PCDATA)>
<!ELEMENT subject (#PCDATA)>
```

An external DTD file has an XML declaration as the first line; the rest is just the same as an internal DTD. To use an external DTD, the document type declaration of the conforming document can take the following form: <!DOCTYPE *root* SYSTEM *"system-identifier"*> where SYSTEM is the keyword informing a parser that an external file is available, and *system-identifier* is the location and filename of the external DTD file. You can use the URL of the DTD file as the system identifier. Let's modify Example 6-1 to use an external DTD.

Edit Example 6-1 (filename: "ex06A.xml"), replacing the internal DTD with a reference to an external file (i.e., "ex06B.dtd," see Example 6-3, line 2), then save it with the filename "ex06C.xml."

Example 6-3: An XML document that uses external DTD – filename: "ex06C.xml"

```
1  <?xml version="1.0" encoding="UTF-8"?>
2  <!DOCTYPE Collection SYSTEM "ex06B.dtd">
3  <?xml-stylesheet type="text/css" href="ex05A.css"?>
4  <Collection>
5  <record >
6      <title>The ugly duckling</title>
7      <creator>Hans Christian Andersen</creator>
8      <subject>Fairy tales</subject>
9      <subject>PZ8.A542</subject>
10 </record>
11 <record>
12     <title>The thief and his master</title>
13     <creator>Jacob Grimm</creator>
14     <creator>Wilhelm Grimm</creator>
15     <subject>Fairy tales</subject>
16     <subject>PZ8.G883</subject>
17 </record>
18 </Collection>
```

In the document type declaration (line 2) and style-sheet processing instruction (line 3) of Example 6-3, only filenames are given for the locations of the reference files, without path or domain information. Therefore, the two files, "ex06B.dtd" and "ex05A.css," must be in the same location (same folder) as Example 6-3.

Remember that the XML declaration of the prolog contains parameters like version and encoding. There is another parameter you may use: standalone. When standalone="yes", no external file is needed to supplement rules specified in the DTD of the current file; when standalone="no", the current document *may* need to retrieve another file to locate necessary rules or additional specifications, say an external DTD file. In these cases, the XML declaration may look like this: <?xml version="1.0" encoding="UTF-8" standalone="no"?>. However, the default value of the standalone parameter is "no", so in principle you don't need to set the parameter explicitly even when you use an external DTD.

SUBSETS

A DTD may combine an internal subset and an external subset. In that case, it may take the following form: <!DOCTYPE *root* SYSTEM *"System-Identifier"* [rules]> where *root* stands for the name of the root element, *System-Identifier* for the location and filename of the external DTD file, and *rules* for internal DTD rules.

Since an external DTD file can be used by many XML documents, you can use a standard DTD as the external DTD subset to provide the general grammar for a class of documents. When you need custom instructions for some of the XML documents covered by your general grammar—for instance, an element not declared in the external DTD—you can add the element type declaration as an internal subset.

NARRATION MIXED WITH METADATA

Let's return to our Hans Christian Andersen example. In some cases, you may want to combine bibliographic data (metadata) with an item's narrative text in the same document, as in example 5-3 (filenames: "ex05C.xml," "ex05E.xml," and "ex05G.xml"). Let's create a DTD for such a document.

Here you will add a document type declaration to "ex05G.xml." Because we haven't yet covered the declaration of attributes in DTDs, let's remove the encoder element from the document for the time being, and save the file with the filename "ex06D.xml" (Example 6-4).

Example 6-4: Andersen's *The Little Match Seller*, encoded in XML with DTD – Filename: "ex06D.xml"

```
<?xml version="1.0" encoding="UTF-8"?>
<!DOCTYPE fairytale        [
<!ELEMENT fairytale        (metadata, maintext)>
```

(cont'd.)

Example 6-4: Andersen's *The Little Match Seller*, encoded in XML with DTD – Filename: "ex06D.xml" ***(Continued)***

```
<!ELEMENT metadata      (descriptive, subject)>
<!ELEMENT descriptive   (title, author*, year?, translator*)>
<!ELEMENT title         (#PCDATA)>
<!ELEMENT year          (#PCDATA)>
<!ELEMENT author        (firstname, middlename?, lastname)>
<!ELEMENT translator    (firstname, middlename?, lastname)>
<!ELEMENT firstname     (#PCDATA)>
<!ELEMENT middlename    (#PCDATA)>
<!ELEMENT lastname      (#PCDATA)>
<!ELEMENT subject       (LCC| DDC| LCSH)*>
<!ELEMENT LCC           (#PCDATA)>
<!ELEMENT DDC           (#PCDATA)>
<!ELEMENT LCSH          (#PCDATA)>
<!ELEMENT maintext      (paragraph)*>
<!ELEMENT paragraph     (#PCDATA | speech)*>
<!ELEMENT speech        (#PCDATA)>
]>
<?xml-stylesheet type="text/css" href="ex05F.css"?>
<fairytale>
<metadata >
   <descriptive>
      <title>The Little Match-Seller</title>
      <author>
         <firstname>Hans</firstname>
         <middlename>Christian</middlename>
         <lastname>Andersen</lastname>
      </author>
      <year>1846</year>
      <translator>
         <firstname>H.</firstname>
         <middlename>P.</middlename>
         <lastname>Paull</lastname>
      </translator>
   </descriptive>
   <subject>
      <LCC>PZ8.A542</LCC>
```

(cont'd.)

Example 6-4: Andersen's *The Little Match Seller*, encoded in XML with DTD – Filename: "ex06D.xml" ***(Continued)***

```
        <LCSH>Fairy tales</LCSH>
    </subject>
</metadata>
<maintext>
<paragraph>It was terribly cold and nearly dark on the last evening of the
old year, and the snow was falling fast. In the cold and the darkness, a
poor little girl, with bare head and naked feet, roamed through the streets.
It is true she had on a pair of slippers when she left home, but they were
not of much use. They were very large, so large, indeed, that they had
belonged to her mother, and the poor little creature had lost them in
running across the street to avoid two carriages that were rolling along at
a terrible rate. One of the slippers she could not find, and a boy seized
upon the other and ran away with it, saying that he could use it as a
cradle, when he had children of his own. So the little girl went on with her
little naked feet, which were quite red and blue with the cold. In an old
apron she carried a number of matches, and had a bundle of them in her
hands. No one had bought anything of her the whole day, nor had anyone
given her even a penny. Shivering with cold and hunger, she crept along;
poor little child, she looked the picture of misery. The snowflakes fell on
her long, fair hair, which hung in curls on her shoulders, but she regarded
them not. </paragraph>
<paragraph>Lights were shining from every window, and there was a
savory smell of roast goose, for it was New-year's eve-yes, she
remembered that. In a corner, between two houses, one of which
projected beyond the other, she sank down and huddled herself together.
She had drawn her little feet under her, but she could not keep off the
cold; and she dared not go home, for she had sold no matches, and could
not take home even a penny of money. Her father would certainly beat
her; besides, it was almost as cold at home as here, for they had only the
roof to cover them, through which the wind howled, although the largest
holes had been stopped up with straw and rags. Her little hands were
almost frozen with the cold. Ah! Perhaps a burning match might be some
good, if she could draw it from the bundle and strike it against the wall,
just to warm her fingers. She drew one out — &#8220;scratch!&#8221;
how it sputtered as it burnt! It gave a warm, bright light, like a little candle,
as she held her hand over it. It was really a wonderful light. It seemed to
the little girl that she was sitting by a large iron stove, with polished brass
feet and a brass ornament. How the fire burned! It seemed so beautifully
warm that the child stretched out her feet as if to warm them, when the
flame of the match went out, the stove vanished, and she had only the
remains of the half-burnt match in her hand. </paragraph>
<paragraph>She rubbed another match on the wall. It burst into a flame,
and where its light fell upon the wall it became as transparent as a veil,
```

(cont'd.)

Example 6-4: Andersen's *The Little Match Seller*, encoded in XML with DTD – Filename: "ex06D.xml" ***(Continued)***

and she could see into the room. The table was covered with a snowy white table-cloth, on which stood a splendid dinner service, and a steaming roast goose, stuffed with apples and dried plums. And what was still more wonderful, the goose jumped down from the dish and waddled across the floor, with a knife and fork in its breast, to the little girl. Then the match went out, and there remained nothing but the thick, damp, cold wall before her. </paragraph>

<paragraph>She lighted another match, and then she found herself sitting under a beautiful Christmas-tree. It was larger and more beautifully decorated than the one which she had seen through the glass door at the rich merchant's. Thousands of tapers were burning upon the green branches, and colored pictures, like those she had seen in the show-windows, looked down upon it all. The little one stretched out her hand towards them, and the match went out. </paragraph>

<paragraph>The Christmas lights rose higher and higher, till they looked to her like the stars in the sky. Then she saw a star fall, leaving behind it a bright streak of fire. <speech>“Someone is dying,”</speech> thought the little girl, for her old grandmother, the only one who had ever loved her, and who was now dead, had told her that when a star falls, a soul was going up to God. </paragraph>

<paragraph>She again rubbed a match on the wall, and the light shone round her; in the brightness stood her old grandmother, clear and shining, yet mild and loving in her appearance. <speech>“Grandmother, ”</speech> cried the little one, <speech>“O take me with you; I know you will go away when the match burns out; you will vanish like the warm stove, the roast goose, and the large, glorious Christmas-tree.”</speech> And she made haste to light the whole bundle of matches, for she wished to keep her grandmother there. And the matches glowed with a light that was brighter than the noon-day, and her grandmother had never appeared so large or so beautiful. She took the little girl in her arms, and they both flew upwards in brightness and joy far above the earth, where there was neither cold nor hunger nor pain, for they were with God. </paragraph>

<paragraph>In the dawn of morning there lay the poor little one, with pale cheeks and smiling mouth, leaning against the wall; she had been frozen to death on the last evening of the year; and the New-year's sun rose and shone upon a little corpse! The child still sat, in the stiffness of death, holding the matches in her hand, one bundle of which was burnt. <speech>“She tried to warm herself,”</speech> said some. No one imagined what beautiful things she had seen, nor into what glory she had entered with her grandmother, on New-year's day. </paragraph>

</maintext>

</fairytale>

All keywords and syntax used in the DTD of Example 6-4 have already been covered under "Internal DTDs" in this chapter. Here is a quick summary.

- <!ELEMENT fairytale (metadata, maintext)> : the fairytale element must contain one metadata element followed by one maintext element.
- <!ELEMENT metadata (descriptive, subject)> : the metadata element must contain one descriptive element followed by one subject element.
- <!ELEMENT descriptive (title, author*, year?, translator*)> : the descriptive element must contain one title element, followed by zero or more author elements, followed by zero or one year element, followed by zero or more translator elements.
- <!ELEMENT title (#PCDATA)>, <!ELEMENT year (#PCDATA)>, <!ELEMENT firstname (#PCDATA)>, <!ELEMENT middlename (#PCDATA)>, <!ELEMENT lastname (#PCDATA)>, <!ELEMENT LCC (#PCDATA)>, <!ELEMENT DDC (#PCDATA)>, <!ELEMENT LCSH #PCDATA)>, <!ELEMENT speech (#PCDATA)> : All the elements declared here can only contain parsed character data as their content, and they can contain no child elements.
- <!ELEMENT maintext (paragraph)*> : the maintext element must contain zero or more paragraph elements as its content.
- <!ELEMENT author (firstname, middlename?, lastname)>, <!ELEMENT translator (firstname, middlename?, lastname)> : the author and translator elements must contain one firstname element, followed by zero or one middlename elements, followed by one lastname element.
- <!ELEMENT paragraph (#PCDATA | speech)*> : the paragraph element can have parsed character data as its content, interspersed with zero or more speech elements.

Since the structure specified by this DTD could well be used to describe a wide array of short fiction, we would do well to maintain it as an external file. Copy the DTD from Example 6-4 and save it as an external DTD file using the filename "ex06E.dtd" (Example 6-5). Change the document type declaration in the prolog of Example 6-4 to <!DOCTYPE fairytale SYSTEM "ex06E.dtd">, and save the file with the filename "ex06F.xml" (Example 6-6) in the same directory as you saved "ex06E.dtd." After parsing, Example 6-4 is practically the same as Example 6-6.

Example 6-5: An external DTD file for fairytale – Filename: "ex6E.dtd"

```
<?xml version="1.0" encoding="UTF-8"?>
<!ELEMENT fairytale          (metadata, maintext)>
<!ELEMENT metadata           (descriptive, subject)>
<!ELEMENT descriptive        (title, author*, year?, translator*)>
<!ELEMENT title              (#PCDATA)>
<!ELEMENT year               (#PCDATA)>
<!ELEMENT author             (firstname, middlename?, lastname)>
<!ELEMENT translator         (firstname, middlename?, lastname)>
<!ELEMENT firstname          (#PCDATA)>
<!ELEMENT middlename         (#PCDATA)>
<!ELEMENT lastname           (#PCDATA)>
<!ELEMENT subject            (LCC| DDC| LCSH)*>
<!ELEMENT LCC                (#PCDATA)>
<!ELEMENT DDC                (#PCDATA)>
<!ELEMENT LCSH               (#PCDATA)>
<!ELEMENT maintext           (paragraph)*>
<!ELEMENT paragraph          (#PCDATA | speech)*>
<!ELEMENT speech             (#PCDATA)>
<!ELEMENT fairytale          (metadata, maintext)>
<!ELEMENT metadata           (descriptive, subject)>
<!ELEMENT descriptive        (title, author*, year?, translator*)>
<!ELEMENT title              (#PCDATA)>
<!ELEMENT year               (#PCDATA)>
<!ELEMENT author             (firstname, middlename?, lastname)>
<!ELEMENT translator         (firstname, middlename?, lastname)>
<!ELEMENT firstname          (#PCDATA)>
<!ELEMENT middlename         (#PCDATA)>
<!ELEMENT lastname           (#PCDATA)>
<!ELEMENT subject            (LCC| DDC| LCSH)*>
<!ELEMENT LCC                 (#PCDATA)>
<!ELEMENT DDC                (#PCDATA)>
<!ELEMENT LCSH               (#PCDATA)>
<!ELEMENT maintext           (paragraph)*>
<!ELEMENT paragraph          (#PCDATA | speech)*>
<!ELEMENT speech             (#PCDATA)>
```

Example 6-6: Using an external DTD for Andersen's *The Little Match Seller* (only the prolog is shown) – Filename: "ex6E.xml"

```
<?xml version="1.0" encoding="UTF-8"?>
<!DOCTYPE     fairytale SYSTEM "ex06D.dtd">
<?xml-stylesheet type="text/css" href="ex05F.css"?>
<fairytale>
...
</fairytale>
```

7 STRUCTURING AN XML DOCUMENT USING ATTRIBUTE LIST DECLARATIONS AND ENTITY DECLARATIONS

Attributes contain additional information pertaining to XML elements. Entities allow you to replace contents in an XML document; they provide a very useful mechanism in real world applications. This chapter teaches you how to declare, define, and use attributes and entities.

ATTRIBUTE LIST DECLARATIONS

As you learned in Chapter 3 (under "Attributes"), an XML element may have attributes that store additional information. You specify what type of attributes an element can have using an attribute list declaration in your DTD. Let's create a DTD with attribute list declarations. In Example 5-2 (filename: "ex05B.xml"), both the record and subject elements have attributes. Edit "ex05B.xml" to add the DTD as shown (Example 7-1, lines 2–16) and save the file with the filename "ex07A.xml." Note that the same style sheet is attached to our document.

Example 7-1: An XML document with attribute list declarations in its DTD – filename: "ex07A.xml"

```
1   <?xml version="1.0" encoding="UTF-8"?>
2   <!DOCTYPE Collection [
3   <!ELEMENT Collection (record)*>
4    <!ELEMENT record     (title | creator | subject)*>
5   <!ATTLIST   record
6      date          CDATA #REQUIRED
7      cataloger     CDATA #REQUIRED
```

(cont'd.)

Example 7-1: An XML document with attribute list declarations in its DTD – filename: "ex07A.xml" ***(Continued)***

```
    recNum      ID      #REQUIRED
>
 <!ELEMENT title (#PCDATA)>
 <!ELEMENT creator (#PCDATA)>
 <!ELEMENT subject (#PCDATA)>
<!ATTLIST subject terms (DDC | LCC | LCSH | UDC | MeSH) #REQUIRED>
]>
<?xml-stylesheet type="text/css" href="ex05A.css"?>
<Collection>
<record recNum="FT-0001" cataloger="Kwong Bor Ng" date="2006-10-24">
   <title>The ugly duckling</title>
   <creator>Hans Christian Andersen </creator>
   <subject terms="LCSH">Fairy tales</subject>
   <subject terms="LCC">PZ8.A542</subject>
</record>
<record recNum="FT-0002" date="2006-11-16" cataloger="Kwong Bor Ng">
   <title>The thief and his master</title>
   <creator>Jacob Grimm</creator>
   <creator>Wilhelm Grimm</creator>
   <subject terms="LCSH">Fairy tales</subject>
   <subject terms="LCC"> PZ8.G883 </subject>
</record>
<record date="2006-12-21" cataloger="Kwong Bor Ng" recNum="RN-0001">
   <title> Notes from the Underground </title>
   <creator>Fyodor Dostoyevsky</creator>
   <subject terms="LCSH">Russia -- Officials and employees -- Fiction.</subject>
   <subject terms="LCC">PG3326.Z4</subject>
</record>
<record recNum="FT-0003" cataloger="Kwong Bor Ng" date="2006-12-22">
   <title>Andersen &amp; his fairytales</title>
   <creator>Hans Christian Andersen </creator>
   <subject terms="LCSH">Fairy tales</subject>
   <subject terms="LCC">PZ8.A542</subject>
</record>
</Collection>
```

An attribute list declaration takes the form <!ATTLIST *element-name attribute-definitions*> where

1. <!ATTLIST is the start delimiter of the declaration;
2. *element-name* identifies the owner element of the attributes;
3. *attribute-definitions* consists of a list of attribute names, attribute types, and attribute default values; and
4. > indicates the end of the declaration.

In Example 7-1, line 5 begins with the start delimiter of an attribute list declaration and then identifies the owner of the attributes, record. Lines 6–8 contain the *attribute-definitions.* There are three such definitions. Each has three components, with the format *attribute-name attribute-type attribute-default.*

1. *Attribute-name* (date, cataloger and recNum) gives the name of the attribute.
2. *Attribute-type* (CDATA and ID) specifies the kind of value the attribute can take.
3. *Attribute-default* (#REQUIRED) defines the default setting.

There is another attribute list declaration in line 13:

```
<!ATTLIST subject terms (DDC | LCC | LCSH | UDC | MeSH) #REQUIRED>
```

In this declaration, the owner element is subject. There is only one attribute definition, with terms as the *attribute-name*, (DDC | LCC | LCSH | UDC | MeSH) as the *attribute-type*, and #REQUIRED as the *attribute-default.*

The following two sections explain the meaning of **attribute type** and **attribute default**.

ATTRIBUTE TYPE

An attribute's type identifies the kinds of values it can contain. There are three attribute types: string, enumerated, and tokenized.

THE STRING ATTRIBUTE TYPE

The string attribute type allows an arbitrary string of characters as its value. The keyword for specifying string-type attributes is CDATA. Its attribute definition takes the form *attribute-name* CDATA *attribute-default.* Don't be confused by this keyword. The value of the attribute is not part of any CDATA section (see Chapter 4, CDATA). It will still be parsed by an XML parser.

In Example 7-1, the cataloger attribute is used to store the name of the creator of the record, and the date attribute is used to store the date the record was created. Their values are ordinary characters (i.e., letters, spaces, dash, and numbers), so these two attributes can be defined as string-type attributes in the attribute list declaration (Example 7-1, lines 6–7).

THE ENUMERATED ATTRIBUTE TYPE

An enumerated-type attribute can only take its value from a list. In the attribute definition, the list is enclosed in a pair of parentheses, and the allowed values in the list are separated by vertical pipes, as in Example 7-1, line 13: <!ATTLIST subject terms (DDC | LCC | LCSH | UDC | MeSH) #REQUIRED>. Here, terms is defined as an enumerated-type attribute of subject, and its value can only be one of the following: DDC, LCC, LCSH, UDC, or MeSH.

TOKENIZED ATTRIBUTE TYPES

Tokenized-type attributes have special constraints on their value. ID and IDREF are two of the most commonly used tokenized type attributes. Let's use them in a demonstration.

The keyword for specifying an ID attribute type is, reasonably enough, ID, and its attribute definition takes the form *attribute-name* ID *attribute-default.* The value of an ID-type attribute must be unique to the entire document, so that it can be used to locate its owner element. In Example 7-1, the recNum attribute of the record element is defined as an ID-type attribute using the keyword ID (line 8), allowing you to assign an identification code to uniquely identify each record (e.g., FT-0001 on line 17, FT-0002 on line 23, etc.)

There are four important constraints for ID attribute types:

1. ID-type attributes must have discrete values regardless of whether they belong to the same element type. This attribute type is used to uniquely identify elements.
2. The value must satisfy the conditions of an XML name (see Chapter 3).
3. An element can have at most one ID-type attribute.
4. An attribute of ID type cannot be an optional attribute.

You can use ID type attributes with IDREF type attributes to create cross references in XML documents. An IDREF type attribute can only use the value of an ID type attribute as its own value. The keyword for specifying an IDREF type attribute is IDREF, and its attribute definition takes the form *attribute-name* IDREF *attribute-default.*

Suppose you want to add a readingList element to Example 7-1 that is designed to contain (1) a grade level (e.g., "low" for K to 6, "high" for 7 to 12), and (2) some recommended works for students of each level. We immediately hit upon a problem. A reading list contains multiple works, so it seems that readingList should be a parent or ancestor of record. On the other hand, a work may belong to multiple reading lists. So what is the proper hierarchical relationship between readingList and record? You can solve this problem using an IDREF-type attribute (Example 7-2, file name: "ex07B.xml").

Example 7-2: An XML document with ID-type and IDREF-type attributes – filename: "ex07B.xml"

```
<?xml version="1.0" encoding="UTF-8"?>
<!DOCTYPE Collection [
   <!ELEMENT Collection (record*, readingList*)>
   <!ELEMENT record  (title | creator | subject)*>
<!ATTLIST        record
   date          CDATA       #REQUIRED
   cataloger     CDATA       #REQUIRED
   recNum        ID          #REQUIRED
>
 <!ELEMENT title (#PCDATA)>
 <!ELEMENT creator (#PCDATA)>
 <!ELEMENT subject (#PCDATA)>
<!ATTLIST subject terms (DDC | LCC | LCSH | UDC | MeSH) #REQUIRED>
   <!ELEMENT   readingList    (item)*>
   <!ATTLIST   readingList    gradeLevel   (low | high)    #REQUIRED>
   <!ELEMENT   item EMPTY>
   <!ATTLIST   item itemNum IDREF #REQUIRED>
]>
<?xml-stylesheet type="text/css" href="ex05A.css"?>
<Collection>
<record recNum="FT-0001" cataloger="Kwong Bor Ng" date="2006-10-24">
   <title>The ugly duckling</title>
   <creator>Hans Christian Andersen </creator>
   <subject terms="LCSH">Fairy tales</subject>
```

(cont'd.)

Example 7-2: An XML document with ID-type and IDREF-type attributes – filename: "ex07B.xml" ***(Continued)***

```
25      <subject terms="LCC">PZ8.A542</subject>
26  </record>
27  <record recNum="FT-0002" date="2006-11-16" cataloger="Kwong Bor Ng">
28      <title>The thief and his master</title>
29      <creator>Jacob Grimm</creator>
30      <creator>Wilhelm Grimm</creator>
31      <subject terms="LCSH">Fairy tales</subject>
32      <subject terms="LCC"> PZ8.G883 </subject>
33  </record>
34  <record date="2006-12-21" cataloger="Kwong Bor Ng" recNum="RN-0001">
35      <title> Notes from the Underground </title>
36      <creator>Fyodor Dostoyevsky</creator>
37      <subject terms="LCSH">Russia -- Officials and employees -Fiction.</subject>
38      <subject terms="LCC">PG3326.Z4</subject>
39  </record>
40  <record recNum="FT-0003" cataloger="Kwong Bor Ng" date="2006-12-22">
41      <title>Andersen &amp; his fairytales</title>
42      <creator>Hans Christian Andersen </creator>
43      <subject terms="LCSH">Fairy tales</subject>
44      <subject terms="LCC">PZ8.A542</subject>
45  </record>
46  <readingList gradeLevel="low">
47      <item itemNum="FT-0001" />
48      <item itemNum="FT-0002" />
49  </readingList>
50  <readingList gradeLevel="high">
51      <item itemNum="RN-0001" />
52  </readingList>
53  </Collection>
```

In Example 7-2, Collection now can have two types of child elements: record and readingList (line 3). A readingList element must have a gradeLevel attribute, which must have either low or high as the attribute value (line 15). A readlingList element can have zero or more item elements as its children (line 14). Although item is defined as an empty element (line 16), it always comes with an IDREF type attribute, which here is itemNum (line 17). All the values of the itemNum attributes (i.e., lines 47, 48, and 51) are from the value of an ID type attribute (i.e., the recNum attributes of record elements on lines 21, 27, and 34.)

Another commonly used tokenized attribute type is NMTOKEN, which allows a combination of any alphanumerical characters, certain ideographic characters, underscore, colon, period, and hyphen as its value. The set of the allowed values is a subset of the values allowed in a CDATA type attribute. In Examples 7-1 and 7-2, the date attribute can be defined as an NMTOKEN type instead of CDATA type because its value is a combination of number and hyphen. However, the cataloger attribute cannot be defined as an NMTOKEN type because its value may contain space, and space is not an allowed character for the value of an NMTOKEN type attribute.

There are other tokenized type attributes, but they are not used that much in the major XML applications of the library world. You can consult Section 3.3.1 of the W3C XML Recommendation (included in the accompanying CD) for a more thorough discussion.

ATTRIBUTE DEFAULT

Attribute default is the last component of an attribute definition. You use it to specify whether an attribute must be present or not, and whether there is a default value. There are three keywords for this specification: (1) **#REQUIRED**, (2) **#FIXED**, and (3) **#IMPLIED**.

#REQUIRED

#REQUIRED means that the attribute must be present whenever its owner element is present. No default value is provided. In Examples 7-1 and 7-2, all attributes have #REQUIRED as their default. Therefore, for every record, gradeLevel, and item element in the document, it must come with the declared attributes.

#FIXED

#FIXED means that there is a default value for the attribute. Whenever you use the keyword #FIXED in an attribute definition, it comes with a quoted string. This quoted string is that default value. In a conforming XML document, if the attribute is provided with the element, it must have the fixed value; if the attribute is not provided with the element, the parser will automatically add it to the element with the fixed value.

In Example 7-1 or 7-2, if you change cataloger CDATA #REQUIRED to cataloger CDATA #FIXED "Kwong Bor Ng" then:

1. For each occurrence of a record element, there should be a cataloger attribute and its value must be Kwong Bor Ng.
2. When there is no cataloger attribute in a record element, an XML parser should automatically supply a cataloger attribute with Kwong Bor Ng as the attribute value.

#IMPLIED

#IMPLIED means that the attribute is optional. You can have it, or you can omit it. In Example 7-1 or 7-2, if you change cataloger CDATA #REQUIRED to cataloger CDATA #IMPLIED, the cataloger attribute will become optional. It is then OK for some record elements to have a cataloger attribute, but other record elements not to have it.

ENTITY

Physically, an XML document can be considered a collection of storage units called entities. An entity can be large, for example, the whole XML document is one entity (the document entity). An entity can be small, for example, there are five predefined entities and they store just one single character (see "Entities and Entity References in Chapter 4).

You can create your own entity using an entity declaration in DTD. In an entity declaration, you specify the name and content of the entity. You invoke an entity using entity reference. An XML parser will parse an entity reference to retrieve its content and use the content to replace the reference in the document. There are two major types of entities: **general entity** and **parameter entity**. General entities are to replace a reference inside a document element, including all of its child elements and descendants. Parameter entities are to replace a reference inside a DTD.

GENERAL ENTITY

General entities are entities for use within the document content. Its entity declaration takes the form <!ENTITY *name "content-for-replacement"*>, where <!ENTITY is the start delimiter, *name* identifies the entity name, and *content-for-replacement* should be replaced by the content you want the entity to store. An entity name must be an XML name (see Chapter 3). You invoke the general entity by using its reference, which has the format &name; (i.e., the name of the entity, delimited by an ampersand sign and a semicolon sign.)

Suppose your library expects to have many records of fairy tales written by Hans Christian Andersen. To save some typing, you can create a general entity with the name HCA to represent Hans Christian Andersen, like this: <!ENTITY HCA "Hans Christian Andersen">. Add the entity declaration (Example 7-3. line 14) to Example 7-1 (filename: “ex07A.xml”). Now you can use the entity reference &HCA; when you need to use the three words Hans Christian Andersen (see Example 7-3, line 20 and line 39). Save the file using the file name “ex07C.xml.” After parsing, “ex07A.xml” is practically the same as “ex07C.xml.”

Example 7-3: An XML document with entity declaration – filename: "ex07C.xml"

```
1   <?xml version="1.0" encoding="UTF-8"?>
2   <!DOCTYPE Collection [
3    <!ELEMENT Collection (record)*>
4    <!ELEMENT record      (title | creator | subject)*>
5   <!ATTLIST    record
6      date        CDATA     #REQUIRED
7      cataloger   CDATA     #REQUIRED
8      recNum      ID        #REQUIRED
9   >
10   <!ELEMENT title (#PCDATA)>
11   <!ELEMENT creator (#PCDATA)>
12   <!ELEMENT subject (#PCDATA)>
13  <!ATTLIST subject terms (DDC | LCC | LCSH | UDC | MeSH) #REQUIRED>
14   <!ENTITY HCA "Hans Christian Andersen">
15  ]>
16  <?xml-stylesheet type="text/css" href="ex05A.css"?>
17  <Collection>
18  <record recNum="FT-0001" cataloger="Kwong Bor Ng" date="2006-10-24">
19     <title>The ugly duckling</title>
20     <creator>&HCA;</creator>
21     <subject terms="LCSH">Fairy tales</subject>
22     <subject terms="LCC">PZ8.A542</subject>
23  </record>
24  <record recNum="FT-0002" date="2006-11-16" cataloger="Kwong Bor Ng">
25     <title>The thief and his master</title>
26     <creator>Jacob Grimm</creator>
27     <creator>Wilhelm Grimm</creator>
28     <subject terms=“LCSH”>Fairy tales</subject>
```

(cont'd.)

Example 7-3: An XML document with entity declaration – filename: "ex07C.xml" ***(Continued)***

```
    <subject terms="LCC"> PZ8.G883 </subject>
</record>
<record date="2006-12-21" cataloger="Kwong Bor Ng" recNum="RN-0001">
    <title> Notes from the Underground </title>
    <creator>Fyodor Dostoyevsky</creator>
    <subject terms="LCSH">Russia -- Officials and employees -- Fiction.</subject>
    <subject terms="LCC">PG3326.Z4</subject>
</record>
<record recNum="FT-0003" cataloger="Kwong Bor Ng" date="2006-12-22">
    <title>Andersen &amp; his fairytales</title>
    <creator>&HCA;</creator>
    <subject terms="LCSH">Fairy tales</subject>
    <subject terms="LCC">PZ8.A542</subject>
</record>
</Collection>
```

EXTERNAL ENTITY

In the above section, the defined entity is an internal entity because there is no separate physical storage object. If you store the content of the entity in a separate file, the entity is an external entity. The entity declaration of an external entity takes the form <!ENTITY *name* SYSTEM *"location-of-file"*> where SYSTEM is the keyword to inform an XML parser that there is an external file. Usually *location-of-file* is the Web address of the external file. If the external file is in the same location (i.e., same directory) as the referencing file, you can just use the filename of the external file as *location-of-file*.

For example, if you have an individual record in its own file (Example 7-4, filename: “ex07D.xml”), you can include it as an external entity in the records collection document.

Example 7-4: An XML file to be used as external entity – filename: "ex07D.xml"

```
<?xml version="1.0" encoding="UTF-8"?>
<record recNum="FT-0004" cataloger="Kwong Bor Ng" date="2006-12-15">
    <title>Little mermaid</title>
    <creator>Hans Christian Andersen </creator>
    <subject terms="LCSH">Fairy tales</subject>
    <subject terms="LCC">PZ8.A542</subject>
</record>
```

Edit Example 7-3 (filename: “ex07C.xml”) to add the external entity declaration (Example 7-5, line 15) and entity reference (Example 7-5, line 44); save the file with the filename “ex07E.xml” in the same directory in which you saved “ex07D.xml.” Your CSS file (Example 7-5, line 17) should also be in the same directory.

Example 7-5: An XML document that uses an external entity – filename: "ex07E.xml"

```
1  <?xml version="1.0" encoding="UTF-8"?>
2  <!DOCTYPE Collection [
3   <!ELEMENT Collection (record)*>
4   <!ELEMENT record       (title | creator | subject)*>
5  <!ATTLIST      record
6      date         CDATA     #REQUIRED
7      cataloger    CDATA     #REQUIRED
8      recNum       ID        #REQUIRED
9  >
10  <!ELEMENT title (#PCDATA)>
11  <!ELEMENT creator (#PCDATA)>
12  <!ELEMENT subject (#PCDATA)>
13 <!ATTLIST subject terms (DDC | LCC | LCSH | UDC | MeSH) #REQUIRED>
14  <!ENTITY HCA "Hans Christian Andersen">
15  <!ENTITY      AF SYSTEM "ex07D.xml">
16 ]>
17 <?xml-stylesheet type="text/css" href="ex05A.css"?>
18 <Collection>
19 <record recNum="FT-0001" cataloger="Kwong Bor Ng" date="2006-10-24">
20     <title>The ugly duckling</title>
21     <creator>&HCA;</creator>
22     <subject terms="LCSH">Fairy tales</subject>
23     <subject terms="LCC">PZ8.A542</subject>
24 </record>
25 <record recNum="FT-0002" date="2006-11-16" cataloger="Kwong Bor Ng">
26     <title>The thief and his master</title>
27     <creator>Jacob Grimm</creator>
28     <creator>Wilhelm Grimm</creator>
29     <subject terms="LCSH">Fairy tales</subject>
30     <subject terms="LCC"> PZ8.G883 </subject>
31 </record>
```

(cont'd.)

Example 7-5: An XML document that uses an external entity – filename: "ex07E.xml"

```
<record date="2006-12-21" cataloger="Kwong Bor Ng" recNum="RN-0001">
   <title> Notes from the Underground </title>
   <creator>Fyodor Dostoyevsky</creator>
   <subject terms="LCSH">Russia -- Officials and employees -- Fiction.</subject>
   <subject terms="LCC">PG3326.Z4</subject>
</record>
<record recNum="FT-0003" cataloger="Kwong Bor Ng" date="2006-12-22">
   <title>Andersen &amp; his fairytales</title>
   <creator>&HCA;</creator>
   <subject terms="LCSH">Fairy tales</subject>
   <subject terms="LCC">PZ8.A542</subject>
</record>
&AF;
</Collection>
```

PARAMETER ENTITY

A general entity is a very useful mechanism for content creation. However, you cannot use a general entity in DTD. In DTD, you use another type of entity to perform the same function: parameter entity. A parameter entity has a slightly different syntax. A parameter entity declaration takes the form <!ENTITY % name "replacement-text">. That is, there is the starting delimiter of an entity declaration, followed by a space; a percent sign; another space; the name of the entity; the text you want to use as replacement, which should be quoted, and finally the right angle bracket, which is the end delimiter of the declaration. A parameter entity reference takes the form %name; instead of &name; .

One of the most common uses of a parameter entity is to store a structure that may be referenced multiple times in a DTD. For example, you can create a parameter entity to store the structure of a personal name and reference it when the structure is needed. In fact, in the area of library cataloging and classification, personal name is a big category because it can play so many different roles: author, translator, illustrator, editor, composer, reviser, compiler, adaptor, etc., and you may want to use the same structure for all of them.

In Example 6-5 (filename: "ex06E.dtd") in the last chapter, there are two personal names in the DTD file, one for author and the other for translator; both of them have the same structure. You can use parameter entity for them (Example 7-6, filename: "ex07F.dtd," note line 7, 8, and 9.) Modify Example 6-6 (filename: "ex06F.xml") to use "ex07F.dtd" as the external DTD, and save the file with filename "ex07G.xml." After

Example 7-6: An external DTD file with a parameter entity – filename: "ex07F.dtd"

```
1   <?xml version="1.0" encoding="UTF-8"?>
2   <!ELEMENT fairytale        (metadata, maintext)>
3   <!ELEMENT metadata         (descriptive, subject)>
4   <!ELEMENT descriptive      (title, author*, year?, translator*)>
5   <!ELEMENT title            (#PCDATA)>
6   <!ELEMENT year             (#PCDATA)>
7   <!ENTITY % pname "firstname, middlename?, lastname">
8   <!ELEMENT author           (%pname;)>
9   <!ELEMENT translator       (%pname;)>
10  <!ELEMENT firstname        (#PCDATA)>
11  <!ELEMENT middlename       (#PCDATA)>
12  <!ELEMENT lastname         (#PCDATA)>
13  <!ELEMENT subject          (LCC| DDC| LCSH)*>
14  <!ELEMENT LCC              (#PCDATA)>
15  <!ELEMENT DDC              (#PCDATA)>
16  <!ELEMENT LCSH             (#PCDATA)>
17  <!ELEMENT maintext         (paragraph)*>
18  <!ELEMENT paragraph        (#PCDATA | speech)*>
19  <!ELEMENT speech           (#PCDATA)>
```

parsing, whether an XML file uses "ex06E.dtd" or "ex07F.dtd" will make little difference.

There is a caveat when you use a parameter entity. In the internal DTD subset, you cannot use parameter entity references **within** markup declarations. This constraint does not apply to external subsets. In Example 7-6, lines 8 and 9, you use parameter entity references within element declarations (i.e., markup declarations). It is OK only because Example 7-6 is an external DTD. It will not work if it is an internal DTD. For an internal DTD, parameter entity references can be used to replace a whole markup declaration but not part of it (i.e., they cannot appear within it).

MARC DTD

A few years ago, when other XML schema languages were not yet very well developed, knowledge-based organizations would use DTDs to create the standard grammars of their encoding languages, for example, MathML

DTD, TEI-Lite DTD, Dublin Core DTD, XHTML DTDs, and MARC DTDs, and others.

Today, there are more options than just DTD, and many of these organizations have switched to schema languages like W3C schema language, Relax NG, and so on. However, it doesn't mean that DTD is already outdated. It has its own merit. Although not as flexible and expressive as some other XML schema languages, in many circumstances DTD is powerful enough to get the job done. For example, the official definitions of XHTML are still specified in multiple DTDs, not in other schema languages.

In the mid 1990s, the Network Development and MARC Standards Office of the Library of Congress developed two DTDs for MARC structures, one for Bibliographic MARC and the other for Authority MARC. Although now if you want to use XML for MARC records, you probably will choose schemas like MARC21Slim, MODS and/or MADS, instead of MARC DTDs, it still will be very beneficial for your understanding of the XML language, especially for its implementation strategy in the library world, if you can read and understand the MARC DTDs.

The original MARC DTDs are very large. The Bibliographic MARC DTD consists of 18,000 lines of code. The Authority MARC DTD consists of more than 8,000 lines of code. Instead of asking you to read the original DTDs, the author of this book has simplified the Bibliographic MARC DTD to less than 2% of the original size and presents it in Appendix 1. It includes all of the necessary MARC fields and subfields for catalog records of monographs, and it is usable for a small collection.

The simplified MARC DTD may serve as a test for you. If you have problems in understanding this DTD, you properly should re-read the previous chapter and this chapter again before moving on to the next chapter.

VALIDITY OF AN XML DOCUMENT

An XML document must be well formed. In addition, a well-formed XML document can be valid. Basically, XML validity requires an XML document to follow the structure and syntax expressed in a grammar, which may be a DTD or schema. If you create an XML document that conforms to a DTD, it is a valid XML document. You will learn about schemas in Part IV of this book.

At this point, you should start to read the formal rules for DTDs in the official XML recommendation, which can be found in the technical report Web site of the W3C Consortium (www.w3.org/TR/). It also appears in the accompanying CD in the "Appendices" folder. In the recommendation, the constraints for creating valid XML documents are marked with the label "Validity Constraint," or simply "VC."

8 NAMESPACES AND THE LIMITATIONS OF DTD

DTDS REVISITED

When XML was first developed, it inherited many characteristics from SGML, including the practice of using DTDs. Although the DTD protocol is a good enough approach for many situations, it does suffer from certain limitations. Among the most infamous of these is its clumsy support of namespaces, which just happens to be a crucial mechanism in the XML language family. It is often impossible to make effective use of XML in a large, complex application without employing namespaces.

This chapter will use the Dublin Core Metadata Element Set (DCMES) as an example while introducing the concept of namespaces and to demonstrate some limitations of the DTD protocol. Don't worry; later chapters will address newer approaches that resolve these limitations.

THE DUBLIN CORE METADATA ELEMENT SET

DCMES is a collection of metadata elements especially designed for the indexing and cataloging of resources. It has been formally endorsed by standards-setting organizations both in the U.S. (National Information Standards Organization [NISO] Z39.85) and the international market (International Standards Organization [ISO] 15836) as the core multidisciplinary metadata element set. DCMES has two levels: Simple and Qualified. Simple Dublin Core consists of fifteen repeatable and optional elements:

1. title : a name given to the resource
2. creator : an entity primarily responsible for making the content of the resource
3. subject : a topic of the content of the resource

4. description : an account of the content of the resource
5. publisher : an entity responsible for making the resource available
6. contributor : an entity responsible for making contributions to the content of the resource
7. date : the date of an event in the life cycle of the resource
8. type : the nature or genre of the content of the resource
9. format : the physical or digital manifestation of the resource
10. identifier : an unambiguous reference to the resource within a given context
11. source : a reference to a resource from which the present resource is derived
12. language : a language in which the intellectual content of the resource is expressed
13. relation : a reference to a related resource
14. coverage : the extent or scope of the content of the resource
15. rights : information about rights held in and over the resource

ENCODING DCMES IN XML DTD

To encode Dublin Core in XML, you can use either a DTD or an XML schema as the validating document. Standard DTDs and schemas of DCMES have been proposed, implemented, and used by various libraries and institutions. Since schemas are more flexible and powerful than DTDs, they are usually used when both protocols are available. When schemas are not used, DTDs should be provided instead. For some applications, it is sensible to provide both schemas and DTDs.

While the XML schema protocol is undoubtedly more powerful and flexible than the DTD standard, schemas are not always the best tool for the job. In situations in which a DTD can provide an acceptably precise, usable document definition, the added complexity involved with creating a schema is a relative detriment. In fact, XHTML, which is now the most widely used text encoding language, is specified in multiple DTDs, not in schemas.

Let's create a DTD for the simple description of DCMES laid out in the list above. In Example 8-1, there are 16 element types declared.

Among them, record must have the other 15 elements as its children, but there is no constraint on their number or the order in which they are listed. All other elements must have parsed character data as their contents. Save the file with the filename: "ex08A.dtd."

Example 8-1: A DTD file for a simple DCMES record – filename: "ex08A.dtd"

```
<?xml version="1.0" encoding="UTF-8"?>
<!ELEMENT record (title | creator | subject | description | publisher | contributor |
date | type | format | identifier | source | language | relation | coverage | rights)*>
<!ELEMENT title (#PCDATA) >
<!ELEMENT creator (#PCDATA) >
<!ELEMENT subject (#PCDATA) >
<!ELEMENT description (#PCDATA) >
<!ELEMENT publisher (#PCDATA) >
<!ELEMENT contributor (#PCDATA) >
<!ELEMENT date (#PCDATA) >
<!ELEMENT type (#PCDATA) >
<!ELEMENT format (#PCDATA) >
<!ELEMENT identifier (#PCDATA) >
<!ELEMENT source (#PCDATA) >
<!ELEMENT language (#PCDATA) >
<!ELEMENT relation (#PCDATA) >
<!ELEMENT coverage (#PCDATA) >
<!ELEMENT rights (#PCDATA) >
```

USING THE DCMES DTD TO CREATE A CATALOG RECORD

Although Example 8-1 is a bare-bones document, it is still a perfectly sound DTD, and you can use it as the external DTD to create conforming DCMES records. Example 8-2 is a DCMES record of Andersen's fairytale *The Emperor's New Suit*. Create the file, save it with the filename "ex08B.xml" in the directory in which you saved "ex08A.dtd." Note that the site "justanexample.edu" (line 20) and the file "Andersen. EmperorsNewSuit.xml" do not exist (line 27) — this is just a fictitious example.

Example 8-2: A simple Dublin Core record of Andersen's *The Emperor's New Suit* – filename: "ex08B.xml"

```xml
<?xml version="1.0" encoding="UTF-8"?>
<!DOCTYPE Collection SYSTEM "ex08A.dtd" [
<!ELEMENT Collection (record*)>
]>
<Collection>
<record>
<title>The emperor's new suit </title>
<creator>Hans Christian Andersen</creator>
<creator>Andersen, H. C. (Hans Christian), 1805-1875.</creator>
<subject>PZ8.A542</subject>
<subject>839.809034</subject>
<subject>Danish literature -- 19th century.</subject>
<subject>Children's literature -- 19th century.</subject>
<subject>Fairy tales -- 19th century.</subject>
<subject>Pride and vanity -- Juvenile fiction.</subject>
<description> A fairy tale written by the Danish writer Hans Christian Andersen
(1805-1875). Two weavers convince the emperor they are making him beautiful new
clothes, visible only to those fit for their posts, but during a royal procession in which
he first wears them, a child whispers that the emperor has nothing on. </description>
<publisher> justanexample.edu </publisher>
<contributor>H. P. Paull </contributor>
<date>1937</date>
<type>World Wide Web resource</type>
<type>electronic resource</type>
<type>text/xml</type>
<format>11 kb</format>
<identifier>http://justanexample.edu/Andersen.EmperorsNewSuit.xml</identifier>
<source>Complete Hans Christian Andersen Fairy Tales</source>
<language>eng </language>
<relation>Browser with XML parser</relation>
<relation>Mode of access: Internet via World Wide Web</relation>
<rights>The only legal and authorized use of this file is for nonprofit production.
The copyright for the file is the sole property of the original owner. </rights>
</record>
</Collection>
```

According to the DCMES guidelines, all DCMES elements are optional and repeatable. For instance, the coverage element is missing from our example. On the other hand, the creator element is used twice. The first use is on line 8, where it records the statement of responsibility (According to *AACR2*, the statement of responsibility of a resource should be transcribed from the chief source of information and need not be expressed in any specific format.) The second use is on line 9, where it stores the author's name, ideally as derived from an authority file.

Example 8-2 is a simple (i.e., unqualified) Dublin Core record. If you wish to include more details, you can use Qualified Dublin Core instead. Qualified Dublin Core allows you to provide a deeper description of each resource. For example, the 15 elements in Simple Dublin Core allow you to provide a nice description of audio files, but they do not provide a convenient or intuitively usable way of indicating the size of such files, their playing length, or the bit rate at which they were encoded. By adding to, or "qualifying," simple Dublin Core, we can provide that information within a widely recognized structure. Qualified Dublin Core also allows you to use controlled vocabularies for the content of the elements: you can require, for example, that each of the six subject elements in lines 10–15 take their values from a controlled vocabulary.

Bear in mind that Dublin Core's great strength is its universality: the more aggressively you customize its basic specification, the more likely it is that some of your metadata will work less than optimally in other people's systems. Visit http://dublincore.org to learn more about Qualified Dublin Core.

NAMESPACES

Choosing names for the elements in your document can be an art unto itself. Names like title or date make perfectly good sense on their own, but within the context of a document, their generality can be problematic. We saw an example of this back in Chapter 1, where title could have been used to indicate Dr. King's honorific or the name of one of his books. In our current example, you may want the processing program to know that the elements in Example 8-2 are not just any title or date, etc., but the title and date from DCMES, which is a widely used scheme. This identification with a known standard ensures that the data stored in your record will be compatible with other records created by other libraries using the same scheme. In XML-speak, you want to specify the **namespace** of the words you use to label items in your document.

Namespaces provide a simple way to qualify element and attribute names by associating them with specific vocabularies. With namespaces you can uniquely identify element and attribute names, allowing elements and attributes with identical names but from different vocabulary schemes to be safely and unambiguously used in the same document. In XML, namespaces are identified using a URI (Uniform Resource Identifier).

URIs are simply strings that identify resources. The URL you use when visiting a Web site is a form of URI. When a URI is used to associate a DTD or schema with a namespace, it uniquely identifies an origin of names available for use in your document. For example, the Dublin Core Metadata Initiative (or DCMI, the organization overseeing DCMES) recommends that all DCMES records use http://purl.org/dc/elements/1.1/ as the namespace URI. Once you associate this namespace URI with your document's elements, there will be no confusion as to their meaning.

Let's add a namespace to Example 8-2. Add an attribute list declaration to Example 8-2, (see Example 8-3, line 4), and save the file with filename "ex08C.xml."

Example 8-3: A simple Dublin Core record of Andersen's *The Emperor's New Suit*, with namespace specification – filename: "ex08C.xml"

```
1  <?xml version="1.0" encoding="UTF-8"?>
2  <!DOCTYPE Collection SYSTEM "ex08A.dtd" [
3  <!ELEMENT Collection (record)>
4  <!ATTLIST record xmln CDATA #FIXED "http://purl.org/dc/elements/1.1/">
5  ]>
6  <Collection>
7  <record>
8  <title>The emperor's new suit </title>
9  <creator>Hans Christian Andersen</creator>
10 <creator>Andersen, H. C. (Hans Christian), 1805-1875.</creator>
11 <subject>PZ8.A542</subject>
12 <subject>839.809034</subject>
13 <subject>Danish literature -- 19th century.</subject>
14 <subject>Children's literature -- 19th century.</subject>
15 <subject>Fairy tales -- 19th century.</subject>
16 <subject>Pride and vanity -- Juvenile fiction.</subject>
17 <description> A fairy tale written by the Danish writer Hans Christian Andersen
18 (1805-1875). Two weavers convince the emperor they are making him beautiful new
19 clothes, visible only to those fit for their posts, but during a royal procession in which
20 he first wears them, a child whispers that the emperor has nothing on. </description>
```

(cont'd.)

Example 8-3: A simple Dublin Core record of Andersen's *The Emperor's New Suit*, with namespace specification – filename: "ex08C.xml" *(Continued)*

```
21  <publisher> justanexample.edu </publisher>
22  <contributor>H. P. Paull </contributor>
23  <date>1937</date>
24  <type>World Wide Web resource</type>
25  <type>electronic resource</type>
26  <type>text/xml</type>
27  <format>11 kb</format>
28  <identifier>http://justanexample.edu/Andersen.EmperorsNewSuit.xml</identifier>
29  <source>Complete Hans Christian Andersen Fairy Tales</source>
30  <language>eng </language>
31  <relation>Browser with XML parser</relation>
32  <relation>Mode of access: Internet via World Wide Web</relation>
33  <rights>The only legal and authorized use of this file is for nonprofit production.
34  The copyright for the file is the sole property of the original owner. </rights>
35  </record>
36  </Collection>
```

The attribute xmlns, appearing in the newly added attribute list declaration, belongs to the record element. Since the keyword #FIXED is used as its default, this attribute can only have one value: http://purl.org/dc/elements/1.1/ (the official namespace URI for DCMES). When there is no such attribute inside the start tag of a record element (as is the case on line 7), an XML parser should automatically supply the xmlns attribute with this fixed value.

xmlns is a special attribute. When an xmlns attribute appears (with no further qualification; see Chapter 9), its value identifies a default namespace URI for its host element and all descendant elements. In effect, now all the DCMES elements in Example 8-3 can be correctly interpreted by an XML processor as elements belonging to the official DCMES namespace.

When you use a default namespace, you don't need to explicitly qualify an element to specify its namespace. The scope of the default namespace extends from the start-tag in which the xmlns attribute appears to the corresponding end-tag, affecting all child elements. All unprefixed element names within its scope belong to the default namespace. This is a handy method in many situations. However, Example 8-3 uses a default namespace only because this is almost the only namespace mechanism a DTD can handle without some sophisticated (or clumsy) circumlocution. DTDs offer almost no support for more nuanced namespace specifications. Many technical references will simply suggest that you use an XML schema instead of a DTD if you need to use namespaces.

LIMITATIONS OF DTDS

Beside namespaces, DTDs suffer from a few other inconveniences and limitations, such as occurrence constraints: you can only specify three occurrence constraints: "zero or more," "zero or one," and "one or more." In Example 8-3, if you use a DTD, you cannot specify an exact number (other than one), a minimum number, or a maximum number for the occurrence of any element.

Another frequently encountered drawback to using DTDs is their very limited support for data-type specifications (dictating that the stored data should be a string, a time duration, a date, a decimal number, a positive integer, etc.). In Example 8-3, it would be nice to specify that the date element must contain a meaningful date or year; using a DTD, we have no way of disallowing a "date" like 12345678 in this element. Furthermore, you cannot create your own data types for situations in which data must be formatted in narrowly defined ways.

Nor do DTDs support sequencing terribly well; for instance, only by dint of clumsy roundabout constructions can a DTD specify an unordered sequence of data. Let's say you want to specify the following: in a record element there can be only three child elements: creator, title and date; each must appear once but their order is insignificant. The element type declaration of record in the DTD will be

```
<!ELEMENT record ((creator, title, date) | (title, creator, date) |
(title, date, creator) | (creator, date, title) | (date, creator, title) |
(date, title, creator)) >
```

With three child elements in the unordered sequence, there are six possible combinations, forcing us to specify the sequence six times. Think about how many combinations would be needed to support the DCMES' 15 possible child elements.

DTDs can provide simple, straightforward specifications of simple, straightforward documents, but because of their inherent limitations, you may want to use a more powerful, flexible approach when specifying the structure and rules governing your content model. XML schemas give you that power and flexibility.

IV ADVANCED XML TECHNIQUES

ASSIGNING STRUCTURE TO AN XML DOCUMENT USING W3C XML SCHEMA LANGUAGE

INTRODUCTION TO SCHEMAS

XML schemas, like DTD, are a formal approach to defining the vocabularies and structure of a class of XML documents. Schemas have many useful mechanisms that are not available in DTD, such as inheritance for elements and user-defined types. With this extra power and flexibility comes an extra degree of complexity, and a complete treatment of schemas is beyond the scope of this book. The focus of this chapter is to give you a solid foundation in XML schema language, enough for you to understand and apply many standard schemas used in the library world. The official recommendations of the W3C Schema language are included in the CD accompanying this book; they are a good starting point for further information after you have finished this chapter.

There are different versions of schema language. Most of the major schemas in the library world use the W3C XML Schema Language. The Metadata Object Description Standard (MODS), the Metadata Authority Description Standard (MADS), Encoded Archival Description (EAD), the Metadata Encoding and Transmission Standard (METS) and NISO Metadata for Images in XML (MIX) are all implemented using the W3C-defined XML Schema Language. Therefore, we will focus on this version, but be aware that there are other equally powerful schema languages. For examples, OpenOffice, DocBook, and the Text Encoding Initiative (TEI) are all successful projects implemented using the Relax NG schema language. To learn more about Relax NG, visit www.relaxng.org.

A SIMPLE SCHEMA

An XML document that conforms to a schema is called an **instance** of the schema. An XML schema is stored in its own file. When you apply it to an XML document, you point to the schema file in the prolog, using a processing instruction. For clarity's sake, let's make a new, simple XML document for our investigation of schemas. Create Example 9-1, and save it with the filename "ex09A.xml."

Example 9-1: An instance document – "ex09A.xml"

```
<?xml version="1.0" encoding="UTF-8"?>
<!-- draft, not the final version yet -->
<author>
<firstname>Hans</firstname>
<middlename>Christian</middlename>
<lastname>Andersen</lastname>
<yearofbirth>1805</yearofbirth>
</author>
```

In Example 9-1, the root element is author. The document should conform to the following structural constraints:

- author can have four children: firstname, middlename, lastname, and yearofbirth.
- firstname, middlename, lastname can only have ordinary text as their contents.
- yearofbirth can only have numbers as its content.
- middlename and yearofbirth are optional inside author. If they appear, they can only appear once.
- The sequential order of the child elements is important; for example, if middlename is present, it must appear after firstname and before lastname.

All of these rules will be described in our schema file. At this point, our schema may look like Example 9-2 (filename: "ex09B.xsd"). Note that this is still a draft toward our final schema, not the finished product.

Example 9-2: An XML schema – filename: "ex09B.xsd"

```
<?xml version="1.0"?>
<!-- draft, not the final version yet. -->
<schema xmlns="http://www.w3.org/2001/XMLSchema">
    <element name="author">
```

(cont'd.)

Example 9-2: An XML schema – filename: "ex09B.xsd" ***(Continued)***

```
5          <complexType>
6             <sequence>
7                <element name="firstname" type="string"/>
8                <element name="middlename" type="string" minOccurs="0"/>
9                <element name="lastname" type="string"/>
10               <element name="yearofbirth" type="gYear"  minOccurs="0"/>
11            </sequence>
12         </complexType>
13      </element>
14   </schema>
```

Looks familiar, doesn't it? Example 9-2 is an XML document in its own right; it uses some special elements and attributes to specify the grammar of a class of documents. The special elements used here are schema, element, complexType, and sequence. The special attributes are name, type, and minOccurs. The elements and attributes are derived from a default namespace, with the URI www.w3.org/2001/XMLSchema (line 3), which is the official namespace URI for XML schemas written in the W3C XML Schema Language. Therefore, the meaning of these elements and attributes, and what should be done with them, must be interpreted and processed according to the rules of the W3C XML Schema Language.

Example 9-2 uses the default namespace method. It can be rewritten as Example 9-3, which uses a prefix (xsd, followed by a colon) to explicitly identify the document's namespace. Let's edit "ex09B.xsd" to match Example 9-3, and save it with the filename "ex09C.xsd." After parsing, Examples 9-2 and 9-3 yield practically the same results. It is standard practice to use the prefixed namespace format when creating schema. The merits of this approach will become apparent when you begin working with multiple namespaces.

Example 9-3: An XML schema with namespace prefixes – filename: "ex09C.xsd"

```
<?xml version="1.0"?>
<!-- draft, not the final version yet. -->
<xsd:schema xmlns:xsd="http://www.w3.org/2001/XMLSchema">
   <xsd:element name="author">
      <xsd:complexType>
```

(cont'd.)

Example 9-3: An XML schema with namespace prefixes – filename: "ex09C.xsd" ***(Continued)***

```
6          <xsd:sequence>
7            <xsd:element name="firstname" type="xsd:string"/>
8            <xsd:element name="middlename" type="xsd:string" minOccurs="0"/>
9            <xsd:element name="lastname" type="xsd:string"/>
10           <xsd:element name="yearofbirth" type="xsd:gYear" minOccurs="0"/>
11         </xsd:sequence>
12       </xsd:complexType>
13     </xsd:element>
14   </xsd:schema>
```

In the following section we will examine Example 9-3 line by line, starting from the namespace declaration (line 3).

To declare a namespace and bind it with a prefix, you need to add a namespace declaration as an attribute to an element using the format: xmlns:*prefix*="namespaceURI". The scope of the namespace starts from the start-tag of the element in which the attribute xmlns:*prefix* appears, and extends to the corresponding end-tag. In Example 9-3, line 3 is a namespace declaration attribute, which is placed inside the start-tag of an element (schema), with xsd as the prefix. From that point on, up to the end-tag of schema, all names prefixed with xsd are associated with the appropriate namespace. Any name with xsd as its prefix belongs to the namespace identified by the official namespace URI for XML schemas written in the W3C XML Schema Language, http://www.w3.org/2001/XMLSchema.

The root element in Example 9-3 is schema, and it carries the xsd prefix. This means that the meaning of this element and of all its descendant elements carrying the same prefix are defined by the W3C XML schema language. This is crucially important: an XML processor will interpret this document and generate output based on its understanding of the language being used. When an XML processor sees that the root element of an XML document is the schema element from the namespace http://www.w3.org/2001/XMLSchema, it knows that the document is an XML schema.

The prefix you use to bind to the namespace URI is a matter of convention. Example 9-3 binds the namespace URI to the prefix xsd only because xsd is the standard designation. You may use whatever prefix you prefer—xs, abc, xyz—but try to keep it simple. What is important here is not the spelling of the prefix, but the namespace URI to which it is bound.

ELEMENT TYPE DECLARATIONS

In Example 9-3, inside the schema element there are four elements, each named element (line 4, and lines 7–10). These are element type declarations.

In an XML schema, you use the element to declare each element type. An element type declaration takes the form <xsd:element … … /> (see Example 9-3, lines 7–10), or <xsd:element … … > … … </xsd:element> (see Example 9-3, lines 4 and 13), where xsd is the prefix for the schema namespace. You can place an element type declaration directly under the schema element (i.e., as its child element) or further down in the document tree as a descendant of the schema element.

If an element type declaration appears directly under the schema element, the declared element is called a **global element**; if it appears further down the document tree, the declared element is called a **local element**. Only global elements can be used as root elements in a schema's instance. When there are multiple global elements declared in a schema, any one of them can be used as the root element in an instance document; the schema file itself does not need to specify which one. In Example 9-3, there is only one global element declared, author. Its declaration is directly under the schema element. Therefore, in an instance of this schema, the root element must be author. The firstname, middlename, lastname, and yearofbirth elements can only appear as child elements of author—none of them can be a root element in an instance document.

Many standard schemas in the library world have multiple global elements. This allows the same schema to be used for different purposes. For example, there are two global elements in the MODS (Metadata Object Description Standard) schema: mods and modsCollection. The former has a structure suitable for one record; the latter has a structure suitable for multiple records. An instance document that uses the MODS schema can choose to use the mods element as its root element to create a record for one item or the modsCollection as its root element to create a collection of records for multiple items. You can visit www.loc.gov/standards to learn more about the MODS schema.

ATTRIBUTES IN ELEMENT TYPE DECLARATIONS

In an XML schema, inside the start-tag of an element type declaration, you can use attributes to define various characteristics of the declared element type. In this section you will learn four of the most commonly used attributes: name, type, minOccurs, and maxOccurs.

USE THE NAME ATTRIBUTE TO ASSIGN AN ELEMENT'S NAME

The name attribute gives a name to the declared element type. In Example 9-3, on line 4, and on lines 7–10, you use the name attributes in the start-tags of five element elements to give names to five element types: author, firstname, middlename, lastname, and yearofbirth.

USE THE TYPE ATTRIBUTE TO SPECIFY A DATA TYPE

The type attribute specifies what kind of content the declared element type can have. There are more than 40 built-in types in the XML Schema Language. Here are some commonly used types:

- anyURI A URI or URL like a Web address
- string Any text string
- decimal Decimal number
- integer Integer number
- gDay Gregorian calendar day of a month, (1, 10, 28, 31).
- gMonth Gregorian calendar month, in other words, integers 1 to 12
- gYear Gregorian calendar year
- time Time in HH:MM:SS-timezone format, for example (13:40:36-05:00)
- date Date in YYYY-MM-DD format (2006-12-31).

When you use the above types in a schema file, you should add the namespace prefix, as in Example 9-3, line 7: <xsd:element name="firstname" type="xsd:string"/>. This declares an element type whose name is firstname and specifies that its content must be in the form of a string of characters.

Using DTDs, you have a very limited number of data types by which to specify content. For example, in a DTD you cannot indicate that a given element always contains a year, but using XML Schema you can specify type="xsd:gYear" (Example 9-3, line 10).

USE THE MINOCCURS AND MAXOCCURS ATTRIBUTES TO SPECIFY OCCURRENCE CONSTRAINTS

Two attributes can be used with the element element to specify occurrence constraints: minOccurs (minimum occurrence) and maxOccurs (maximum occurrence). If these are not present, their values will be set by default to "1" by an XML parser. If you wish there to be no limit on the number of occurrences of a given element, use maxOccurs="unbound".

In Example 9-3, for the element type declaration of the middlename (line 8) and yearofbirth (line 10), minOccurs equal 0 and there is no maxOccurs attribute, so on a practical level these are the same as using question mark (the notation for zero or one occurrence) in a DTD. The only difference is that in a DTD you would specify the occurrence constraints on child elements when you declare the parent element. In schema, you specify the occurrence constraints directly in the child element declaration.

DEFINE YOUR OWN DATA TYPE

XML elements are essentially storage units for data. The XML Schema Language acknowledges two kinds of elements: those that have **complex types** and those that have **simple types**. If an element has child elements or attributes, it has a complex type. If an element has no child elements and no attributes, it has a simple type. In Example 9-3, firstname, middlename, lastname, and yearofbirth can only store string characters and year—because they cannot store child elements or attributes, they have simple types. On the other hand, the author element contains child elements, so it has a complex type.

In an XML schema file, declaring an element type involves specifying what kind of data it can store by assigning an existing data type as the value of the type attribute of the element element: for example, type="xsd:string", or type="xsd:gYear", as demonstrated in subsection "Use the Type Attribute to Specify a Data Type" in this chapter. The value of the type attribute must be a name of an existing data type. When there is no existing data type that fits the storage structure, you can define your own new data type by using the simpleType element (used for defining a simple type storage unit) or the complexType element (used for defining a complex type storage unit). The syntax used by each of these special elements is quite similar.

In Example 9-3, because there is no existing data type that fits the storage structure of author, the element type declaration of author does not have a type attribute (unlike the element type declarations of firstname, middlename, lastname, and yearofbirth). Instead, Example 9-3 creates a new data type using the complexType element (line 5).

The complexType element defines the structure of a new data type by using different child elements and attributes. The following are some examples.

SEQUENCE, CHOICE, AND ALL

Under the complexType element, if you use the sequence child element, like this,

```
<xsd:complexType>
   <xsd:sequence>
      <xsd:element name="x" ...  ... />
      <xsd:element name="Y" ...  ... />
      <xsd:element name="Z" ...  ... />
   </xsd:sequence>
</complexType>
```

you specify that in an instance document, the element that has this type must have an ordered sequence of child elements as its content, like this:

```
<X> ...  ... </X>
<Y> ...  ... </Y>
<Z> ...  ... </Z>
```

If you use the choice child element, as in this example,

```
<complexType>
   <xsd:choice>
      <xsd:element name="X" ...  ... />
      <xsd:element name="Y" ...  ... />
      <xsd:element name="Z" ...  ... />
   </xsd:choice>
</complexType>
```

you specify that the element that has this type must have one and only one child element, which must be an X element, a Y element, or a Z element.

If you use the all child element, like this,

```
<complexType>
   <xsd:all>
      <xsd:element name="x" ...  ... />
```

```
        <xsd:element name="Y" ... ... />
        <xsd:element name="Z" ... ... />
    </xsd:all>
</complexType>
```

you specify that the element that has this type must contain elements X, Y and Z as its content, but that their order of appearance is insignificant.

ATTRIBUTES

There are multiple ways to declare attributes in a schema. One of them is to use the attribute element. By using the attribute element as a child element under the complexType element, you specify that any element that has this type must carry the corresponding attribute.

For example, if you want to specify that an author element must have an email_address attribute, you add the following line into the schema: <xsd:attribute name="email_address" type="xsd:string" use="required"/>, like so:

```
<element name="author">
    <complexType>
        <sequence>
            ... ...
        </sequence>
        <xsd:attribute name="email_address" type="xsd:string"
        use="required"/>
    </complexType>
</element>
```

Now, in an instance document of this schema, each author element must have an email_address attribute. If you want the attribute to be optional, change use="required" to use="optional".

SIMPLECONTENT AND COMPLEXCONTENT

The W3C XML Schema Language acknowledges two basic kinds of content: (1) an element that can have only text as its content is said to have simple content; (2) an element that can also have child element(s) as its content is said to have complex content. Note that whether the content of an element is simple or complex does not depend on whether it has attributes or not. Therefore, an element can have complex type and simple content at the same time if it has attributes but no child element.

When you define your new data type, you can use the simpleContent child element or complexContent child element to specify what kind of content the new data type will have. The type definition in Example 9-3 (lines 5–12) has complex content because the content consists of four child elements (i.e., firstname, middlename, lastname. and yearofbirth). Accordingly, the element type declarations of the four child elements should be inside the complexContent child element, like this:

```
<complexType>
  <complexContent>
    <xsd:sequence>
      <xsd:element name="firstname" type="xsd:string"/>
      <xsd:element name="middlename" type="xsd:string"
      minOccurs="0"/>
      <xsd:element name="lastname" type="xsd:string"/>
      <xsd:element name="yearofbirth" type="xsd:gYear"
      minOccurs="0"/>
    </xsd:sequence>
  </complexContent>
</complexType>
```

However, an XML parser will have no problem in processing the type definition correctly even if you omit the complexContent element, since by definition any element serving as a parent to other elements contains complex content. In obvious, straightforward situations like these, the syntax of XML Schema language allows you to simply omit the complexContent element.

To derive a new type based on an existing type, you should not use this abbreviated approach. If you intend to create a type that has simple content, use the simpleContent element inside the type definition. If you are going to create a new type that has complex content, use the complexContent element inside the type definition.

For example, if in the instance document you want to have elements like this:

```
<title level="beginner"> Introduction to ABC </Title>
<title level="expert"> Advanced ABC </Title>
```

You *cannot* declare the title element to be of type xsd:string in the schema file, as in <xsd:element name="title" type="xsd:string"/>, because xsd:string is a simple type, and an element that has simple type cannot carry attributes. The title element itself has a complex type (because it has an attribute), but contains simple content (because it has character data as its content, not child elements). The most precise way of reflecting this arrangement is to derive a new complex type based on an existing simple data type. In the schema file, you can use the complexType element and the simpleContent element to declare the title element, like this:

```
<xsd:element name="title">
   <xsd:complexType>
      <xsd:simpleContent>
         <xsd:extension base="xsd:string">
            <xsd:attribute name="level" type="string"/>
         </xsd:extension>
      </xsd:simpleContent>
   </xsd:complexType>
</xsd:element>
```

When you derive new type based on an existing type, the derivation can be done either by an extension element or by using a restriction element. In the above, we have an extension element. If you want to add more element(s) and/or attribute(s) to an existing type to derive a new type, you can use the extension element and set its base attribute to the existing type. Conversely, if you want to reduce the range of elements and attributes available to an existing class to create a new, more conceptually focused class, you would use the restriction element and set its base attribute the same way.

ANONYMOUS AND NAMED TYPES

When you create a new data type, you can assign a name to it. If there is no name assigned, it is called an anonymous type definition. Example 9-3 uses the complexType element to define a data type for the author element. This new type is not assigned a name. Therefore, the type definition is an anonymous type definition. The anonymous type definition in Example 9-3 starts with line 5 and ends at line 12.

Anonymous type definitions are often used when the data type will not be re-used in the same schema document. If there are other element type declarations in the schema that will use the same type, you can give the type a name so that you can re-use it simply by using the type attribute of the element element. Only when a type has a name can you refer to it via the type attribute of the element element. Let's demonstrate this with an example. Create Example 9-4, and save it with the filename: "ex09D.xsd."

Example 9-4: An XML schema with a named type – filename: "ex09D.xsd"

```
1   <?xml version="1.0"?>
2   <!-- draft, not the final version yet -->
3   <xsd:schema xmlns:xsd="http://www.w3.org/2001/XMLSchema">
4       <xsd:element name="author" type="pnameType"/>
5       <xsd:complexType name="pnameType">
6           <xsd:sequence>
7               <xsd:element name="firstname" type="xsd:string"/>
8               <xsd:element name="middlename" type="xsd:string" minOccurs="0"/>
9               <xsd:element name="lastname" type="xsd:string"/>
10              <xsd:element name="yearofbirth" type="xsd:gYear" minOccurs="0"/>
11          </xsd:sequence>
12      </xsd:complexType>
13  </xsd:schema>
```

In Example 9-4, a type appropriate to personal names is defined using the complexType element. Line 5 reads <xsd:complexType name="pname-Type">, which means that (1) you are defining a new type, (2) this new type is a complex type, and (3) the name of this new type is pnameType. Lines 6 through 11 contain the type definition, which is exactly the same as the anonymous type definition for author in Example 9-3. However, note the hierarchical position of the complexType element. In Example 9-3, it is a child element of an element element, while in Example 9-4 it is no longer a child element of the element element but a child element of the schema element. This change is significant because it makes the type definition a global definition instead of an inline definition. The defined type becomes a global type, usable by any element in the document. Anonymous types are usually defined inline; named types are usually defined globally.

The pnameType type is a globally defined type customized to fit the structure of a personal name. Now that it has been established, you can use it in other places of the same schema. If any other element takes a personal name as its content—author's name, translator's name, cataloger's name, etc.—you can use pnameType as the value of the type attribute in the element declaration (i.e., type="pnameType"), just like line 4 of Example 9-4.

TARGET NAMESPACES

When you create a schema, you are really creating new vocabularies (element types, attributes, and named data types, etc.) that can be used in instance documents. These vocabularies belong to a namespace, which is called the target namespace of the schema.

In a schema file, you specify the target namespace to be a particular URI (or URL) using the targetNamespace attribute of the schema element. In an instance document, you use the namespace declaration attribute (i.e., xmlns:*prefix* = "namespaceURI") to associate a prefix with the same URI, and then assign the prefix to all the vocabularies coming from the schema.

When there are multiple schemas used in an instance document, you use multiple namespace declaration attributes in the instance document to associate different prefixes with different namespace URIs. The namespace URIs used in the declarations in the instance document should be identical to the target namespace URIs specified in the corresponding schema document. Using this mechanism, there will be no confusion no matter how many schemas you use in the same instance document.

Let's use the schema you have just created to demonstrate the use of target namespaces. Suppose your library decides to use the URI "http://justanexample.org/personalName/1.0/" as the target namespace of the schema. You can add this information to your schema file by adding the targetNamespace attribute to the schema element, like this: targetNamespace="http://justanexample.org/personalName/1.0/" (Example 9-5, line 4). After the addition, all elements, attributes, and types that are declared and defined in the schema element belong to this namespace. Now your schema file should look like Example 9-5 (filename: "ex09E.xsd")...but it is not quite done yet.

Example 9-5: An (incomplete) XML schema with a target namespace – filename: "ex09E.xsd"

```
1   <?xml version="1.0"?>
2   <!-- draft, not finished yet, you may get an error warning when you save the file -->
3   <xsd:schema xmlns:xsd="http://www.w3.org/2001/XMLSchema"
4       targetNamespace="http://justanexample.edu/personalName/1.0/">
5       <xsd:element name="author" type="pnameType"/>
6       <xsd:complexType name="pnameType">
7           <xsd:sequence>
8               <xsd:element name="firstname" type="xsd:string"/>
9               <xsd:element name="middlename" type="xsd:string" minOccurs="0"/>
10              <xsd:element name="lastname" type="xsd:string"/>
11              <xsd:element name="yearofbirth" type="xsd:gYear" minOccurs="0"/>
12          </xsd:sequence>
13      </xsd:complexType>
14  </xsd:schema>
```

When schema has the targetNamespace attribute, all of the vocabularies (element, attribute, type, etc.) declared and defined in the schema file now belong to a particular namespace. When you use these vocabularies, even in the same document, you need to specify the namespace to which each belongs.

In Example 9-5, when the elements and types are from the W3C XML Schema Language, they have the xsd prefix, so an XML parser will understand how to interpret them. There is a vocabulary in the file that an XML parser will not intuitively understand: the pnameType used on line 5. On line 5, the document declares an element type with the name author and indicates that the content of an author element should have a structure of pnameType. What, wonders our parser, is pnameType? What structure should it have?

The schema contains a type definition with the name pnameType. This data type belongs to the target namespace of the schema because it is part of a vocabulary created by the schema. However, an XML parser does not know the pnameType *used* on line 5 is the same as the pnameType *defined* in lines 6–13. There is no information about the namespace of the pnameType used on line 5. It may come from another set of vocabularies (i.e., another namespace). You need to specify that the namespace of the data type used in the type attribute of the element type declaration of author is identical with the target namespace of this schema.

Edit "ex09E.xsd" to add a namespace prefix to the value of the type attribute inside the element type declaration of author, like Example 9-6, and save it with the filename "ex09F.xsd."

Example 9-6: An XML schema with a target namespace – filename: "ex09F.xsd"

```
1   <?xml version="1.0"?>
2   <xsd:schema xmlns:xsd="http://www.w3.org/2001/XMLSchema"
3       xmlns:pn="http://justanexample.edu/personalName/1.0/"
4       targetNamespace="http://justanexample.edu/personalName/1.0/">
5       <xsd:element name="author" type="pn:pnameType"/>
6       <xsd:complexType name="pnameType">
7           <xsd:sequence>
8               <xsd:element name="firstname" type="xsd:string"/>
9               <xsd:element name="middlename" type="xsd:string" minOccurs="0"/>
10              <xsd:element name="lastname" type="xsd:string"/>
11              <xsd:element name="yearofbirth" type="xsd:gYear" minOccurs="0"/>
12          </xsd:sequence>
13      </xsd:complexType>
14  </xsd:schema>
```

Note that there are two new additions in Example 9-6: a namespace declaration attribute (line 3) and the prefix pn (line 5). In the namespace declaration attribute, the prefix pn is bound to a namespace URI, which is the same as the target namespace URI. Now, when an XML parser sees pn:pnameType (line 5), it knows that this pnameType is the same as the pnameType defined later in the same schema because they have the same name *and* belong to the same namespace.

ASSOCIATING AN INSTANCE DOCUMENT WITH ITS SCHEMA

To validate an instance document against its schema, an XML parser needs to know where to find the schema file. To help this process along, you can store the location of a document's schema by using an attribute from a special namespace: the schemaLocation attribute from the namespace specified by the URI "http://www.w3.org/2001/XMLSchema-instance". This attribute has two components: (1) the namespace URI of the schema, and (2) the location of the schema file, which usually is a URL. This URL can either be a relative or an absolute Web address. The two components are enclosed in the same set of quotation marks and are separated by white space.

Suppose you want to specify that the schema with the target namespace "http://justanexample.edu/personalName/1.0/" can be retrieved from the same directory as the instance document with the filename "ex09F.xsd." You can make this association by adding the following two attributes to the root element of the instance document:

```
xmlns:xsi="http://www.w3.org/2001/XMLSchema-instance"
xsi:schemaLocation="http://justanexample.edu/personalName/1.0/
ex09F.xsd"
```

The xmlns:xsi attribute is a namespace declaration. It associates the namespace "http://www.w3.org/2001/XMLSchema-instance" with the xsi prefix. Adding this attribute allows us to use vocabularies from the "http://www.w3.org/2001/XMLSchema-instance" namespace, which allows us to use the schemaLocation attribute from this namespace in the second attribute.

The xsi:schemaLocation attribute specifies two properties. The first is the target namespace of the schema, http://justanexample.edu/personalName/1.0/. The second is the location of the schema file, expressed as a relative URL. The two properties are enclosed in the same set of quotation marks and separated by white space.

In an instance document, when using vocabularies from a schema, you should include a namespace declaration attribute to the start-tag of the element the first time a given vocabulary is used (or earlier, in an ancestor element). For example, before you use any vocabulary from the schema "ex09F.xsd" in an instance document, add the xmlns:*prefix* attribute to the root element, like so: xmlns:pn="http://justanexample.edu/personalName/1.0/". This allows you to use the prefix pn throughout the entire instance document. Note that namespace URI used in the xmlns:pn attribute of the instance document should be identical to the target namespace URI of the schema. Example 9-7 (filename: "ex09G.xml") is an instance document conforming to the schema "ex09F.xsd." Note the three attributes of the root element (on lines 3, 4, and 5).

Example 9-7: An instance XML document conforming to the schema "ex09F.xsd" – filename: "ex09G.xsd"

```
1  <?xml version="1.0" encoding="UTF-8"?>
2  <pn:author
3     xmlns:pn="http://justanexample.edu/personalName/1.0/"
4     xmlns:xsi="http://www.w3.org/2001/XMLSchema-instance"
5     xsi:schemaLocation="http://justanexample.edu/personalName/1.0/   ex09F.xsd">
6     <firstname>Hans</firstname>
7     <middlename>Christian</middlename>
8     <lastname>Andersen</lastname>
9     <yearofbirth>1805</yearofbirth>
10 </pn:author>
```

For Example 9-7 to be correct, both the instance document ("ex09G.xml") and its schema file ("ex09F.xsd") should be in the same folder of the same machine. To use a schema located on another machine owned by another organization, you would simply change the value of the xsi:schemaLocation attribute to the URL of the schema file. For example, if the schema is accessible by the URL http://someOrganization.org/ex09F.xsd, as in Example 9-7, the value of the xsi:schemaLocation attribute would become:

```
xsi:schemaLocation="http://justanexample.edu/personalName/1.0/
   http://someOrganization.edu /DepartmentX/SectionY/ex08E.xsd"
```

Although you see two URLs in the value of the xsi:schemaLocation attribute, the first URL doesn't need to point to a real Web site or Web page. It is a namespace URI, representing an abstract space to which all the vocabularies created by the schema belong, not an actual Web site. On the other hand, the second URL must point to a file—the file of the schema itself—so that an XML processor can retrieve the schema file to validate the instance document.

A MORE FLEXIBLE APPROACH TO SCHEMA CREATION

There is only one global element type declared in the schema "ex09F.xsd": author. Because author is the only global element in the schema, any instance document conforming to this schema must use author as its root element. This is quite restrictive. A more flexible approach is to declare multiple global elements and leave it up to the user to pick the appropriate one as the root element. Edit "ex09F.xsd" (Example 9-6) so it looks like Example 9-8, then save it with the filename "ex09H.xsd."

Example 9-8: Another approach to creating our schema – filename: "ex09H.xsd"

```
<?xml version="1.0"?>
<xsd:schema xmlns:xsd="http://www.w3.org/2001/XMLSchema"
          xmlns:pn="http://justanexample.edu/personalName/1.0/"
          targetNamespace="http://justanexample.edu/personalName/1.0/">
   <xsd:element name="author" type="pn:pnameType"/>
   <xsd:complexType name="pnameType">
      <xsd:sequence>
         <xsd:element ref="pn:firstname"/>
         <xsd:element ref="pn:middlename" minOccurs="0"/>
         <xsd:element ref="pn:lastname"/>
         <xsd:element ref="pn:yearofbirth" minOccurs="0"/>
      </xsd:sequence>
   </xsd:complexType>
   <xsd:element name="firstname" type="xsd:string"/>
   <xsd:element name="middlename" type="xsd:string"/>
   <xsd:element name="lastname" type="xsd:string"/>
   <xsd:element name="yearofbirth" type="xsd:gYear"/>
</xsd:schema>
```

In Example 9-8, there are five global element types declared: author, firstname, middlename, lastname, and yearofbirth. They are all global element types because all of them are direct children of the xsd:schema element.

For the definition of the user-defined data type pnameType, our old schema used four (local) element declarations contained inside xsd:sequence, with type attributes. In our new schema, instead of using the type attributes, the ref attributes are used to refer to the four global elements. You can use the ref attribute because all four of these local elements will have the same type as their global equivalences, but just as you have the prefix pn on line 5, you need to add the same prefix on lines 8, 9, 10, and 11.

Here there are five global elements—five elements declared immediately under the schema element. Since any global element can be used as a root element in an instance document, the flexibility of the previous schema is dramtically extended. Because the schema is still quite simple, the long-range benefits of this flexibility might not be immediately apparent. So make the schema a bit more interesting. Modify Example 9-8 so it looks like Example 9-9, and save it with the filename "ex09Ixsd."

Example 9-9: A schema with more global elements – filename: "ex09I.xsd"

```
<?xml version="1.0"?>
<xsd:schema xmlns:xsd="http://www.w3.org/2001/XMLSchema"
        xmlns:pn="http://justanexample.edu/personalName/1.0/"
        targetNamespace="http://justanexample.edu/personalName/1.0/"
        elementFormDefault="qualified">
    <xsd:element name="author" type="pn:pnameType"/>
    <xsd:element name="translator" type="pn:pnameType"/>
    <xsd:element name="cataloger" type="pn:pnameType"/>
    <xsd:complexType name="pnameType">
        <xsd:sequence>
            <xsd:element ref="pn:firstname"/>
            <xsd:element ref="pn:middlename" minOccurs="0"/>
            <xsd:element ref="pn:lastname"/>
            <xsd:element ref="pn:yearofbirth" minOccurs="0"/>
        </xsd:sequence>
    </xsd:complexType>
    <xsd:element name="firstname" type="xsd:string"/>
    <xsd:element name="middlename" type="xsd:string"/>
    <xsd:element name="lastname" type="xsd:string"/>
    <xsd:element name="yearofbirth" type="xsd:gYear"/>
</xsd:schema>
```

Compare this revision to the schema in Example 9-8; there are now two more global element declarations: translator and cataloger. This schema can now also be used for instance documents with translator or cataloger as their root elements. Since, in the definition of the pnameType, the minOccurs attribute of the local yearofbirth element is set to 0, you can simply omit this local element if you think it is unnecessary to record the year of birth for a translator or cataloger.

One more special attribute has been added inside the schema element in Example 9-9: the attributeFormDefault attribute on line 5. When this attribute is set to "qualified", all the local elements in an instance document should have prefixes to qualify their namespaces. In other words, if you want to use Example 9-7 (filename: "ex09G.xml") with the schema "ex09I.xsd," you need to modify the instance document to match Example 9-10 (filename: "ex09J.xml").

Example 9-10: An XML document that conforms to Example 9-9 – filename: "ex09J.xml"

```
1   <?xml version="1.0" encoding="UTF-8"?>
2   <pn:author
3       xmlns:pn="http://justanexample.edu/personalName/1.0/"
4       xmlns:xsi="http://www.w3.org/2001/XMLSchema-instance"
5       xsi:schemaLocation="http://justanexample.edu/personalName/1.0/   ex09I.xsd">
6       <pn:firstname>Hans</pn:firstname>
7       <pn:middlename>Christian</pn:middlename>
8       <pn:lastname>Andersen</pn:lastname>
9       <pn:yearofbirth>1805</pn:yearofbirth>
10  </pn:author>
```

There are only two differences between Example 9-7 (filename: "ex09G.xml") and the schema in Example 9-10 (filename: "ex09J.xml"). The first difference is the location of the schema (see the xsi:schemaLocation attribute on line 5). In Example 9-7, the schema file used is "ex09F.xsd"; in Example 9-10, the schema file used is "ex09I.xsd." The second difference has to do with local elements. Since you are now using the schema file "ex09I.xsd," in which the elementFormDefault attribute is set to "qualified", all the local elements (i.e., the firstname, middlename, lastname, and yearofbirth elements) in Example 9-10 must be qualified, in this case by pn prefixes.

FROM DTD TO SCHEMA

In the previous chapters, we used a DTD instead of a schema to govern the structure of our fairytale document. Example 9-11 is such a DTD.

Example 9-11: An external DTD file for a fairytale – filename: "ex09K.dtd"

```
<?xml version="1.0" encoding="UTF-8"?>
<!ELEMENT fairytale (metadata, maintext)>
<!ELEMENT metadata (encoder, descriptive, subject)>
<!ENTITY % pname "firstname, middlename?, lastname">
<!ELEMENT encoder ((%pname;), comment*)>
<!ATTLIST encoder email_address CDATA #REQUIRED>
<!ELEMENT comment (#PCDATA)>
<!ELEMENT descriptive (title, author+, year?, translator*)>
<!ELEMENT subject (LCC | DDC | LCSH)*>
<!ELEMENT LCC (#PCDATA)>
<!ELEMENT DDC (#PCDATA)>
<!ELEMENT LCSH (#PCDATA)>
<!ELEMENT title (#PCDATA)>
<!ELEMENT author (%pname;)>
<!ELEMENT translator (%pname;)>
<!ELEMENT year (#PCDATA)>
<!ELEMENT maintext (paragraph*)>
<!ELEMENT paragraph (#PCDATA | speech)*>
<!ELEMENT speech (#PCDATA)>
<!ELEMENT firstname (#PCDATA)>
<!ELEMENT middlename (#PCDATA)>
<!ELEMENT lastname (#PCDATA)>
```

Everything shown in Example 9-11 is covered in Chapters 6 and 7.

Now let's convert our DTD into a schema. There are a few different approaches you can take to perform the translation; one of them is shown in Example 9-12 (filename: "ex09L.xsd").

Example 9-12: The fairytale DTD converted to a schema – filename: "ex09L.xsd"

```
<?xml version="1.0" encoding="UTF-8"?>
<xsd:schema xmlns:xsd="http://www.w3.org/2001/XMLSchema"
    xmlns:ft="http://justanexample.edu/fairytale/"
    targetNamespace="http://justanexample.edu/fairytale/"
    elementFormDefault="qualified">
  <xsd:element name="fairytale">
    <xsd:complexType>
      <xsd:sequence>
        <xsd:element ref="ft:metadata"/>
        <xsd:element ref="ft:maintext"/>
      </xsd:sequence>
    </xsd:complexType>
  </xsd:element>
  <xsd:element name="metadata">
    <xsd:complexType>
      <xsd:sequence>
        <xsd:element ref="ft:encoder"/>
        <xsd:element ref="ft:descriptive"/>
        <xsd:element ref="ft:subject"/>
      </xsd:sequence>
    </xsd:complexType>
  </xsd:element>
  <xsd:complexType name="pnameType">
    <xsd:sequence>
      <xsd:element name="firstname" type="xsd:string"/>
      <xsd:element name="middlename" type="xsd:string" minOccurs="0"/>
      <xsd:element name="lastname" type="xsd:string"/>
    </xsd:sequence>
    </xsd:complexType>
  <xsd:element name="encoder">
    <xsd:complexType>
      <xsd:complexContent>
        <xsd:extension base="ft:pnameType">
          <xsd:sequence>
            <xsd:element name="comment" type="xsd:string"
              minOccurs="0" maxOccurs="unbounded"/>
          </xsd:sequence>
```

(cont'd.)

Example 9-12: The fairytale DTD converted to a schema – filename: "ex09L.xsd"
(Continued)

```
            <xsd:attribute name="email_address" type="xsd:string" use="required"/>
          </xsd:extension>
        </xsd:complexContent>
      </xsd:complexType>
    </xsd:element>
    <xsd:element name="descriptive">
      <xsd:complexType>
        <xsd:sequence>
          <xsd:element name="title" type="xsd:string"/>
          <xsd:element ref="ft:author" maxOccurs="unbounded"/>
          <xsd:element name="year" type="xsd:gYear" minOccurs="0"
            maxOccurs="unbounded"/>
          <xsd:element ref="ft:translator" minOccurs="0" maxOccurs="unbounded"/>
        </xsd:sequence>
      </xsd:complexType>
    </xsd:element>
    <xsd:element name="subject">
      <xsd:complexType>
        <xsd:choice minOccurs="0" maxOccurs="unbounded">
          <xsd:element name="LCC" type="xsd:string"/>
          <xsd:element name="DDC" type="xsd:string"/>
          <xsd:element name="LCSH" type="xsd:string"/>
        </xsd:choice>
      </xsd:complexType>
    </xsd:element>
    <xsd:element name="author" type="ft:pnameType"/>
    <xsd:element name="translator" type="ft:pnameType"/>
    <xsd:complexType name="maintext">
      <xsd:sequence>
        <xsd:element ref="ft:paragraph" minOccurs="0" maxOccurs="unbounded"/>
      </xsd:sequence>
    </xsd:complexType>
    <xsd:element name="maintext">
      <xsd:complexType>
        <xsd:sequence>
          <xsd:element ref="ft:paragraph" minOccurs="0" maxOccurs="unbounded"/>
```

(cont'd.)

Example 9-12: The fairytale DTD converted to a schema – filename: "ex09L.xsd" *(Continued)*

```
         </xsd:sequence>
      </xsd:complexType>
   </xsd:element>
   <xsd:element name="paragraph">
      <xsd:complexType mixed="true">
         <xsd:choice minOccurs="0" maxOccurs="unbounded">
            <xsd:element name="speech" type="xsd:string"/>
         </xsd:choice>
      </xsd:complexType>
   </xsd:element>
</xsd:schema>
```

Carefully compare Examples 9-11 and 9-12 to see how the specifications written in one language are phrased in another. All of the syntax used in Example 9-12 has been discussed in this chapter, which means that it is still new to you. If you have problems understanding Example 9-12, reviewing this chapter should help. Example 9-13 (filename: "ex09M.xml") is an instance document that conforms to Example 9-12.

Example 9-13: An instance document that conforms to the fairytale schema – filename: "ex09M.xml"

```
<?xml version="1.0" encoding="UTF-8"?>
<ft:fairytale  xmlns:ft="http://justanexample.edu/fairytale/"
   xmlns:xsi="http://www.w3.org/2001/XMLSchema-instance"
   xsi:schemaLocation="http://justanexample.edu/fairytale/   ex09L.xsd">
<ft:metadata>
      <ft:encoder email_address="kwongbor@gmail.com">
         <ft:firstname>Kwong</ft:firstname>
         <ft:middlename>Bor</ft:middlename>
         <ft:lastname>Ng</ft:lastname>
      </ft:encoder>
      <ft:descriptive>
         <ft:title>The Little Match-Seller</ft:title>
         <ft:author>
            <ft:firstname>Hans</ft:firstname>
```

(cont'd.)

Example 9-13: An instance document that conforms to the fairytale schema – filename: "ex09M.xml" ***(Continued)***

```xml
            <ft:middlename>Christian</ft:middlename>
            <ft:lastname>Andersen</ft:lastname>
         </ft:author>
         <ft:year>1846</ft:year>
         <ft:translator>
            <ft:firstname>H.</ft:firstname>
            <ft:middlename>P.</ft:middlename>
            <ft:lastname>Paull</ft:lastname>
         </ft:translator>
      </ft:descriptive>
      <ft:subject>
         <ft:LCC>PZ8.A542</ft:LCC>
         <ft:LCSH>Fairy tales</ft:LCSH>
      </ft:subject>
   </ft:metadata>
<ft:maintext>
      <ft:paragraph>It was terribly cold and nearly dark on the last evening of the old year, and the snow was falling fast. In the cold and the darkness, a poor little girl, with bare head and naked feet, roamed through the streets. It is true she had on a pair of slippers when she left home, but they were not of much use. They were very large, so large, indeed, that they had belonged to her mother, and the poor little creature had lost them in running across the street to avoid two carriages that were rolling along at a terrible rate. One of the slippers she could not find, and a boy seized upon the other and ran away with it, saying that he could use it as a cradle, when he had children of his own. So the little girl went on with her little naked feet, which were quite red and blue with the cold. In an old apron she carried a number of matches, and had a bundle of them in her hands. No one had bought anything of her the whole day, nor had anyone given her even a penny. Shivering with cold and hunger, she crept along; poor little child, she looked the picture of misery. The snowflakes fell on her long, fair hair, which hung in curls on her shoulders, but she regarded them not. </ft:paragraph>
      <ft:paragraph>Lights were shining from every window, and there was a savory smell of roast goose, for it was New-year's eve—yes, she remembered that. In a corner, between two houses, one of which projected beyond the other, she sank down and huddled herself together. She had drawn her little feet under her, but she could not keep off the cold; and she dared not go home, for she had sold no matches, and could not take home even a penny of money. Her father would certainly beat her; besides, it was almost as cold at home as here, for they had only the roof to cover them, through which the wind howled, although the largest holes had been stopped up with straw and rags. Her little hands were almost frozen with the cold. Ah! perhaps a burning match might be some good, if she could draw it from the bundle and strike it against the wall, just to warm her
```

(cont'd.)

Example 9-13: An instance document that conforms to the fairytale schema – filename: "ex09M.xml" *(Continued)*

fingers. She drew one out—<ft:speech>“scratch!”</ft:speech> how it sputtered as it burnt! It gave a warm, bright light, like a little candle, as she held her hand over it. It was really a wonderful light. It seemed to the little girl that she was sitting by a large iron stove, with polished brass feet and a brass ornament. How the fire burned! and seemed so beautifully warm that the child stretched out her feet as if to warm them, when the flame of the match went out, the stove vanished, and she had only the remains of the half-burnt match in her hand. </ft:paragraph>

<ft:paragraph>She rubbed another match on the wall. It burst into a flame, and where its light fell upon the wall it became as transparent as a veil, and she could see into the room. The table was covered with a snowy white table-cloth, on which stood a splendid dinner service, and a steaming roast goose, stuffed with apples and dried plums. And what was still more wonderful, the goose jumped down from the dish and waddled across the floor, with a knife and fork in its breast, to the little girl. Then the match went out, and there remained nothing but the thick, damp, cold wall before her. </ft:paragraph>

<ft:paragraph>She lighted another match, and then she found herself sitting under a beautiful Christmas-tree. It was larger and more beautifully decorated than the one which she had seen through the glass door at the rich merchant's. Thousands of tapers were burning upon the green branches, and colored pictures, like those she had seen in the show-windows, looked down upon it all. The little one stretched out her hand towards them, and the match went out. </ft:paragraph>

<ft:paragraph>The Christmas lights rose higher and higher, till they looked to her like the stars in the sky. Then she saw a star fall, leaving behind it a bright streak of fire. <ft:speech>“Someone is dying,”</ft:speech> thought the little girl, for her old grandmother, the only one who had ever loved her, and who was now dead, had told her that when a star falls, a soul was going up to God. </ft:paragraph>

<ft:paragraph>She again rubbed a match on the wall, and the light shone round her; in the brightness stood her old grandmother, clear and shining, yet mild and loving in her appearance. <ft:speech>“Grandmother,”</ft:speech> cried the little one, <ft:speech>“O take me with you; I know you will go away when the match burns out; you will vanish like the warm stove, the roast goose, and the large, glorious Christmas-tree.”</ft:speech> And she made haste to light the whole bundle of matches, for she wished to keep her grandmother there. And the matches glowed with a light that was brighter than the noon-day, and her grandmother had never appeared so large or so beautiful. She took the little girl in her arms, and they both flew upwards in brightness and joy far above the earth, where there was neither cold nor hunger nor pain, for they were with God. </ft:paragraph>

<ft:paragraph>In the dawn of morning there lay the poor little one, with pale cheeks and smiling mouth, leaning against the wall; she had been frozen to death on the last evening of the year; and the New-year's sun rose and shone upon a little corpse! The child still sat, in the stiffness of death, holding the matches in her hand, one bundle of which was burnt. <ft:speech>“She tried to warm herself,”</ft:speech> said some. No one imagined what beautiful things she had seen, nor into what glory she had entered with her grandmother, on New-year's day. </ft:paragraph>

</ft:maintext> </ft:fairytale>

Following the success of the DTDs for Bibliographic MARC and Authority MARC, the Library of Congress developed a flexible and extensible schema in the W3C XML Schema Language. Called MARC 21 SLIM, it can be used to represent a complete MARC record in XML. If you are interested in learning more about this schema, please read Appendix 2, "The MARC21 SLIM Schema."

After you have finished reading this chapter, you may want to read the XML Schema Recommendations. The XML Schema Recommendations are divided into three parts. The first part is a primer on various XML Schema concepts. The second part defines all of the structures used in XML Schemas. The third part describes the data types used by XML Schemas. You can visit the technical reports Web site of the W3 Consortium to look for the three documents (www.w3.org/TR). They are also included in the accompanying CD under the folder "Appendices," with the file names "TheXMLSchemaPart0.pdf," "TheXMLSchemaPart1.pdf," and "TheXMLSchemaPart2.pdf."

10 TRANSFORMING XML DOCUMENTS USING EXTENSIBLE STYLESHEET LANGUAGE

COMPONENTS OF XSL

In Chapter 5, you learned how to apply presentational instructions to XML files using a style language called CSS. Along with CSS, there is another style language available for use with XML documents, one that is more advanced and powerful than its forebear: Extensible Stylesheet Language (XSL). There are three major components of XSL.

XSLT (XSL Transformations): A language used to transform a source XML document into another desired structure, for example, from XML to HTML, or from an instance document based on one schema to another instance document based on another schema. The structure of the resulting document can be very different from the structure of the source document: existing elements and content can be reordered and filtered, and new elements and content can be added.

XPath: A language that can access any node of an XML document accurately. XPath is used to navigate through the elements, attributes, processing instructions, and other units of an XML document to retrieve information.

XML-FO (XML Formatting Objects): A language that specifies the semantics of output formats for different media (browsers, printers, cell phones, etc.). Initially, XSLT and XSL-FO were developed together as a single standard, but they were later separated into two initiatives.

In this chapter, we will focus on using XSLT to transform XML documents into HTML documents for Web display. This transformation can be performed on the client side, in which case the XML documents with their corresponding XSLT files are rendered by each user's Web browser. The transformation can also be performed on the server side, in which case a scripting language like PHP or ASP parses the appropriate files and generates the desired product on-the-fly before sending it back to the requesting browser. You will see examples for both approaches in this chapter.

XSLT TEMPLATES

Let's jump right in with a simple XSLT style sheet consisting of one single rule. The rules in an XSLT style sheet are called templates. An XSLT file can be thought of as a collection of templates. In an XSLT file, each template is a template element from the XSL Transformations namespace. It consists of two components: (1) A pattern, and (2) A sequence of things to do when the pattern is matched.

Create Example 10-1 (filename: "ex10A.xsl") using either a text editor or an XML editor.

Example 10-1: A very simple XSL file – filename: "ex10A.xsl"

```
1  <?xml version="1.0" encoding="UTF-8"?>
2  <xsl:stylesheet version="1.0"
3            xmlns:xsl="http://www.w3.org/1999/XSL/Transform">
4     <xsl:template match="ft:fairytale"
5            xmlns:ft="http://justanexample.edu/fairytale/">
6     This is a fairy tale.
7     </xsl:template>
8  </xsl:stylesheet>
```

In Example 10-1, the root element is a stylesheet element, which is bound to the official XSL Transformations namespace URI (http://www.w3.org/1999/XSL/Transform), identifying the document as a W3C XSLT stylesheet. By convention, most XSLT style sheets use xsl as the prefix for the XSL Transformations namespace.

In an XSLT style sheet, you can use either one of the two elements from the XSL Transformations namespace as root element: the stylesheet element or the transform element. These two elements are completely synonymous (see Section 2.2 of the XSLT specification, which is an official W3C recommendation. To access the document, visit the technical report Web site of the W3 Consortium, www.w3.org/TR. It is also included in the accompanying CD under the "Appendices" folder, file name "XSLT.pdf").

Therefore, lines 2 and 8 of Example 10-1 can be rewritten as

```
<xsl:transform version="1.0"
xmlns:xsl="http://www.w3.org/1999/XSL/Transform">
... ...
</xsl:transform>
```

In addition to the declaration of the XSL Transformations namespace, there is another namespace declaration in Example 10-1, xmlns:ft="http://justanexample.edu/fairytale/," which must be present the first time (or before) you use the prefix ft to represent a namespace.

There is only one rule present in Example 10-1. It associates a condition, match="ft:fairytale", with an instruction, This is a fairy tale. When this style sheet is applied to a source XML document, the XML processor will check the names of all elements in the source document against the style sheet. Specifically, the processor will try to match the source document's element names with the value of the template element's match attribute (in this case, "ft:fairytale") found in the style sheet. Once it sees an ft:fairytale element in the source document, it will print the appropriate text string, This is a fairy tale, into the result document. Using XML terminologies, the same process can be described this way: when a pattern is matched with a node in a source document tree, the sequence constructor (the content of the template) is instantiated, and the result will be written out to the result tree.

You can use a Web browser to apply an XSLT style sheet to an XML source file. Most of the major Web browsers (Internet Explorer 6 or above, Netscape Navigator 7.1 or above, Mozilla 1.4 or above, FireFox 1.0 or above, etc.) have a built-in client-side XSLT processing ability.

You can demonstrate this process using the fairytale file from the last chapter (Example 9-13, filename: "ex09M.xml"). Since there is no style sheet file associated with "ex09M.xml," if you use a Web browser to view the file, you will only see the document tree.

Link the style sheet file "ex10A.xsl" to "ex09M.xml" by adding the following processing instruction after the XML declaration and before the root element (i.e., ft:fairytale) of the source document ("ex09M.xml"): <?xml-stylesheet type="text/xsl" href="ex10A.xsl"?>.

Save the source file as "ex10B.xml." Also, copy the corresponding schema file "ex09L.xsd" and paste it as "ex10C.xsd." Change the xsi:schemaLocation attribute in the root element of "ex10B.xml" to point to "ex10C.xsd" instead of "ex09L.xsd." Instead of xsi:schemaLocation= "http://justanexample.edu/fairytale/ ex09B.xsd" you should now have xsi:schemaLocation="http://justanexample.edu/fairytale/ ex10C.xsd". When you make the change, remember that the value of the xsi:schemaLocation attribute should have two components. There must be a white space between the namespace URI and the location of the schema file. Now the file "ex10B.xml" should look like Example 10-2.

Example 10-2: Use the simple XSL file – filename: "ex10B.xml"

```
<?xml version="1.0" encoding="UTF-8"?>
<?xml-stylesheet type="text/xsl" href="ex10A.xsl"?>
```

(cont'd.)

Example 10-2: Use the simple XSL file – filename: "ex10B.xml" ***(Continued)***

```
<ft:fairytale  xmlns:ft="http://justanexample.edu/fairytale/"
          xmlns:xsi="http://www.w3.org/2001/XMLSchema-instance"
          xsi:schemaLocation="http://justanexample.edu/fairytale/
             ex10C.xsd">
<ft:metadata> ...  ... </ft:metadata>
<ft:maintext>
   <paragraph> ...  ... </paragraph>
          ...  ...
   <paragraph> ...  ... </paragraph>
</ft:maintext>
</ft:fairytale>
```

Example 10-2 has one more processing instruction than Example 9-13 (filename: "ex09M.xml"): <?xml-stylesheet type="text/xsl" href="ex10A.xsl"?>. However, if you view "ex10B.xml" through a Web browser, you will see much less content: either you see only one line of text, This is a fairy tale, or you will see nothing at all, just an empty document.

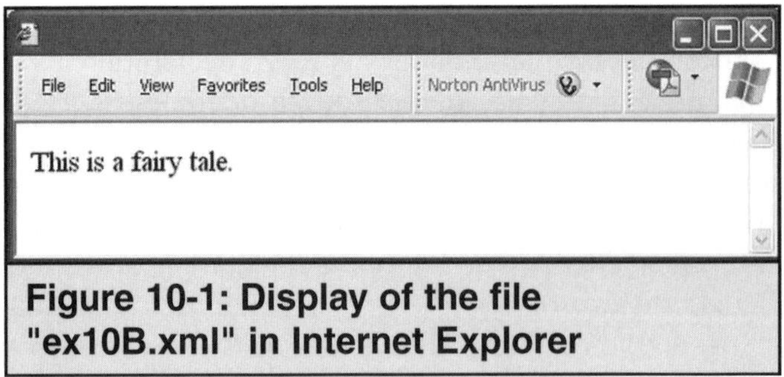

Figure 10-1: Display of the file "ex10B.xml" in Internet Explorer

In the XSLT style sheet file "ex10A.xsl," there is only one template: If there is a ft:fairytale element, print the text string This is a fairytale. A Web browser will execute the rule when its XSLT processor sees the ft:fairytale element in the source document, and it will produce the text string "This is a fairy tale" as output. All the content and children of the ft:fairytale element in the source file will be ignored. The output will be shown in the browser window (as in Figure 10-1) if the browser is able to display plain text in the absence of HTML code. Some browsers will not display text when there is no HTML tagging; through those browsers, you will see only an empty window.

If there is no match between the root element and the condition specified in the template, all the contents of the root element, including the contents of all its descendant elements, will be displayed as text. For example, if the only rule in the file "ex10A.xsl" is <xsl:template match="ABC"> Something Here! </xsl:template>, there will be no match between "ex10B.xml" and the rule because there is no ABC element in "ex10B.xml." When you view "ex10B.xml," it will look like Figure 10-2.

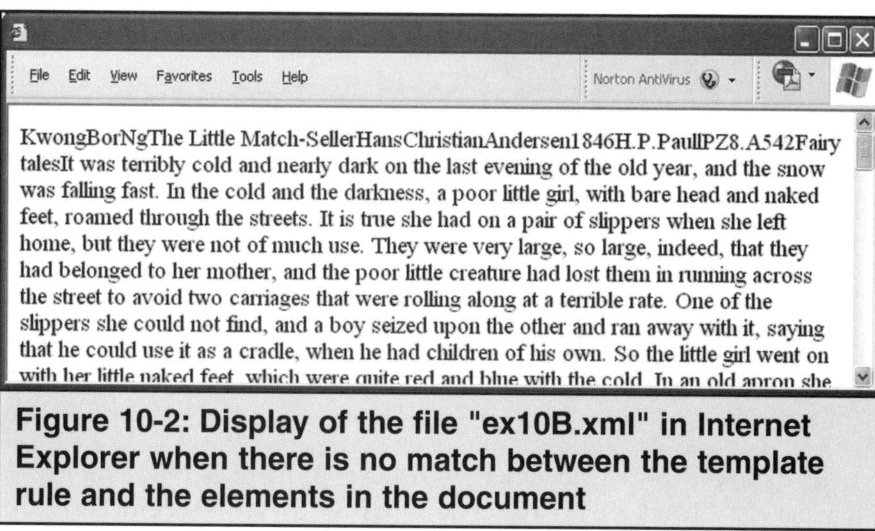

Figure 10-2: Display of the file "ex10B.xml" in Internet Explorer when there is no match between the template rule and the elements in the document

In Figure 10-2, no formatting niceties are added, not even spaces between the contents of different elements. The XSLT engine in the browser simply spills out the contents of every element within "ex10B.xml" without any further formatting.

OUTPUTTING HTML CODES

Your next task is to make the fairy tale's presentation more palatable to its readers. First of all, instruct the transformation to generate some basic HTML code that is designed to provide a basic visual structure to the resulting Web page. There are multiple ways to do this: for example, you can use an optional attribute of the xsl:output element called method: <output method="html"/>. Or you can enter the HTML code you need directly into the XSL file.

Add the appropriate instructions to "ex10A.xsl," as in Example 10-3, and save it with the filename "ex10D.xsl."

Example 10-3: An XSL file that outputs HTML codes – filename: "ex10D.xsl"

```
1   <?xml version="1.0" encoding="UTF-8"?>
2   <xsl:stylesheet version="1.0"
3           xmlns:xsl="http://www.w3.org/1999/XSL/Transform">
4     <xsl:template match="ft:fairytale"
5           xmlns:ft="http://justanexample.edu/fairytale/">
6       <html>
7       <head><title>Andersen's Fairytale</title></head>
8       <body bgcolor="aliceblue">
9       <font color="darkblue" face="Georgia, Arial" size="16pt">
10      <xsl:apply-templates />
11      </font>
12      </body>
13      </html>
14    </xsl:template>
15  </xsl:stylesheet>
```

In Example 10-3 (filename: "ex10D.xsl"), there is one template. It contains (1) a block of HTML code (lines 6–13), with specifications for the page title, background color, font color, font face, and font size; and (2) an XSL element, xsl:apply-template (line 10), which is placed inside the HTML body. Using this style sheet, when an XSL processor sees an element ft:fairytale from the source XML document, the specified block of HTML code will be generated and printed to the resulting document. To demonstrate how this affects the resulting HTML document, we will use an unusually large font size of 16 points (line 9).

The xsl:apply-template element (line 10) is called an instruction element. It instructs an XSL processor to move on to the children (child elements, attributes, texts, even comments or processing instructions) of the matched node to see whether any other templates apply to them. Since no other template exists in the style sheet, an XSL processor will not find a match—it will simply spill out the contents of all the child elements, as in Figure 10-2. However, this time, there will be a light blue background, and the text will be rendered in the Georgia font, colored dark blue, and quite large in size. If you don't have the xsl:apply-template element and you link the XSLT style sheet to the fairy tale file, you will see an empty page when you use an XSL-compliant browser to view the fairy tale file.

Edit the file "ex10B.xml" to link it to "ex10D.xsl" instead of to "ex10A.xsl." That is, instead of <?xml-stylesheet type="text/xsl" href= "ex10A.xsl"?>, you should have <?xml-stylesheet type="text/xsl" href= "ex10D.xsl"?>. Save the file with the filename "ex10E.xml." When you view this file in a browser with the XSLT style sheet file "ex10D.xsl" in the same folder as "ex10E.xml," it should look like Figure 10-3.

Figure 10-3: Display of the file "ex10E.xml" in Internet Explorer

THE VALUE-OF ELEMENT AND THE SELECT ATTRIBUTE

In "ex10D.xsl," there is only one template; there are no other templates to apply when the instruction element (xsl:apply-templates) is invoked. Let's add some more templates. Edit "ex10D.xsl" to match Example 10-4, and save the file using the file name "ex10F.xsl."

Example 10-4: An XSLT style sheet with two templates – filename: "ex10F.xsl"

```
<?xml version="1.0" encoding="UTF-8"?>
<xsl:stylesheet version="1.0"
   xmlns:xsl="http://www.w3.org/1999/XSL/Transform"
   xmlns:ft="http://justanexample.edu/fairytale/">
   <xsl:template match="ft:fairytale">
      <html>
         <head><title>Andersen's Fairytale</title></head>
            <body bgcolor="aliceblue">
               <font color="darkblue" face="Georgia, Arial">
                  <xsl:apply-templates />
               </font>
```

(cont'd.)

Example 10-4: An XSLT style sheet with two templates – filename: "ex10F.xsl" *(Continued)*

```
12              </body>
13          </html>
14      </xsl:template>
15  <xsl:template match="ft:descriptive">
16  <h1 align="center"><xsl:value-of select="ft:title" /></h1>
17  <h2 align="center"><xsl:value-of select="ft:author" /></h2>
18  <h3 align="center"><xsl:value-of select="ft:year" /></h3>
19  </xsl:template>
20  </xsl:stylesheet>
```

Example 10-4 (filename: "ex10F.xsl") has the following modifications and additions:

The position of the namespace declaration: In "ex10D.xsl," the namespace declaration of the prefix ft is attached to the xsl:template element when the ft prefix is used the first time (Example 10-3, line 5). In "ex10F.xsl," it is attached to the xsl:style element before the ft prefix is used (Example 10-4, line 4). Namespaces can be declared the first time the corresponding namespace prefix is used. Alternatively, a namespace may be declared in an ancestor of the element you wish to affect before its prefix is used. Each of these approaches is valid when used properly. However, as Example 10-4 shows, if you attach the namespace declaration to the first xsl:template element (as Example 10-3), you must declare it again in the second xsl:template element. Therefore, instead of declaring the namespace the first time the prefix ft is used, we declare it in an ancestor element of all xsl:template elements, in this case the xsl:style element.

The font size specification: In Example 10-4, the HTML block contains no font size specification. In Example 10-3, there is a size attribute with the unusually large value of 16 points.

The second template: There is a second template in "ex10F.xsl" (lines 15–19). The matching pattern of the template is "ft:descriptive". This contains three instructions that an XSLT processor should carry out when an ft:descriptive element is seen in the source document (lines 16–18). In the instructions, the xsl:value-of element is used to retrieve the value or content of a node, and the select attribute is used to identify the node. Based on the three instructions, an XSLT processor will retrieve the contents of three child elements (ft:title, ft:author, and ft:year) of the ft:descriptive element, and print them out to the resulting document with different HTML heading levels assigned to each (h1, h2, and h3, respectively).

If no xsl:apply-templates element is present in the first template, this second template will not be instantiated. When you view the resulting document through a Web browser, you will see an empty page. However, if you lack both the xs:apply-template element *and* the entire first template, the second template will be instantiated when the XSLT processor sees the ft:descriptive element in the source document.

Edit "ex10E.xml" to link it to "ex10F.xsl." That is, instead of <?xml-stylesheet type="text/xsl" href="ex10D.xsl"?>, you should have <?xml-stylesheet type="text/xsl" href="ex10F.xsl"?>. Save the file with the filename "ex10G.xml."

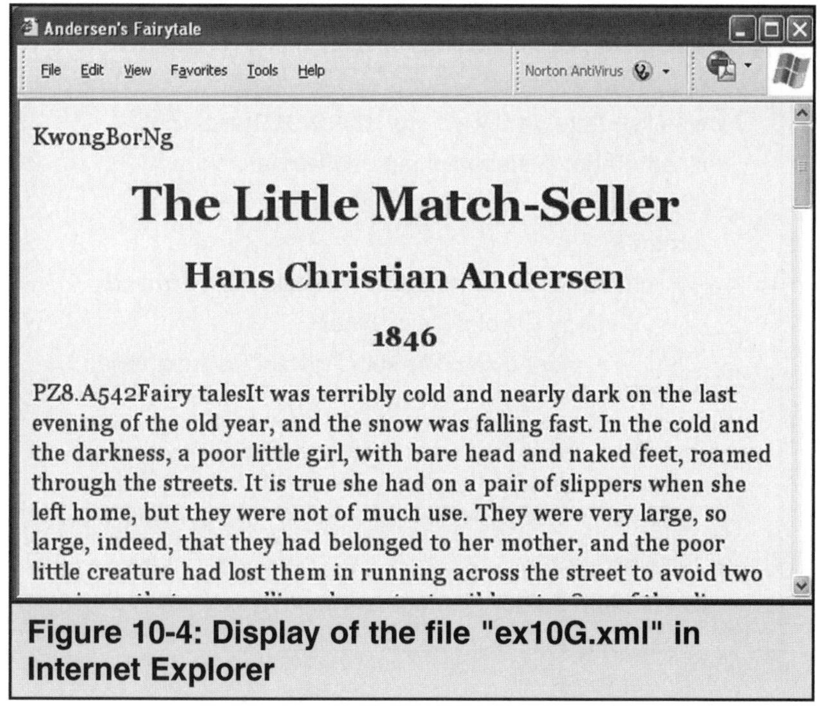

Figure 10-4: Display of the file "ex10G.xml" in Internet Explorer

Use a Web browser to view "ex10G.xml" (with "ex10F.xsl"); it should look like Figure 10-4. The first line of display is the name of the encoder without any spaces separating the first, middle, and last names. The body of the text consists of one big paragraph, with the classification number and subject heading printed together. We have this somewhat cramped result because we have provided no specific instructions about what to do with the contents of the ft:fairytale element when the first template is activated with the instruction element xsl:apply-templates; there is no select attribute. In "ex10F.xsl," the only specific instruction is in the second template, which specifies the HTML codes (i.e., h1, h2, and h3) that should be printed with the content of the ft:title, ft:author, and ft:year elements when the ft:descriptive element is encountered. The title, author, and year are nicely displayed, but not the rest of the document.

CONTEXT NODE AND TEXT NODE

Edit “ex10F.xsl” to match Example 10-5, and save the file using the filename “ex10H.xsl.”

Example 10-5: An XSLT style sheet with multiple templates – filename: "ex10H.xsl"

```
1  <?xml version="1.0" encoding="UTF-8"?>
2  <xsl:stylesheet version="1.0"
3    xmlns:xsl="http://www.w3.org/1999/XSL/Transform"
4    xmlns:ft="http://justanexample.edu/fairytale/">
5    <xsl:template match="ft:fairytale">
6      <html>
7        <head><title>Andersen's Fairytale</title></head>
8          <body bgcolor="aliceblue">
9            <font color="darkblue" face="Georgia, Arial">
10             <xsl:apply-templates />
11           </font>
12         </body>
13     </html>
14   </xsl:template>
15   <xsl:template match="ft:metadata">
16     <xsl:apply-templates select="ft:descriptive"/>
17   </xsl:template>
18   <xsl:template match="ft:descriptive">
19     <h1 align="center"><xsl:value-of select="ft:title" /></h1>
20     <h2 align="center"><xsl:value-of select="ft:author" /></h2>
21     <h3 align="center"><xsl:value-of select="ft:year" /></h3>
22   </xsl:template>
23   <xsl:template match="ft:paragraph">
24     <p align="justify"><xsl:value-of select="." /> </p>
25   </xsl:template>
26 </xsl:stylesheet>
```

Example 10-5 has two new templates. The first new template is described in lines 15–17. The matching pattern here is the ft:metadata element. Based on it, when an XSLT processor sees an ft:metadata element from the source document, it should apply only the rules that are specified for the ft:descriptive element. Accordingly, except for the ft:title, ft:author, and ft:year elements, which are selected in the template of the ft:descriptive element, other descendant elements of the ft:metadata element will not be processed.

The second new template is described in lines 23–25. The matching pattern here is the ft:paragraph element. The period in the select attribute is an expression in the XPath language. It stands for the content of the currently matched node (in this case, a context node). Based on this template, when an XSLT processor sees an ft:paragraph element in the source document, it should output the content of the ft:paragraph element as text into the resulting document, with the HTML code <p> enclosing the text content. In other words, there will be a nice paragraph break.

Edit “ex10G.xml” to use “ex10H.xsl” instead of “ex10F.xsl”. Save it with the filename “ex10I.xml.” When you use a Web browser to view “ex10G.xml” with “ex10H.xsl” in the same folder as “ex10I.xml,” it should look like Figure 10-5.

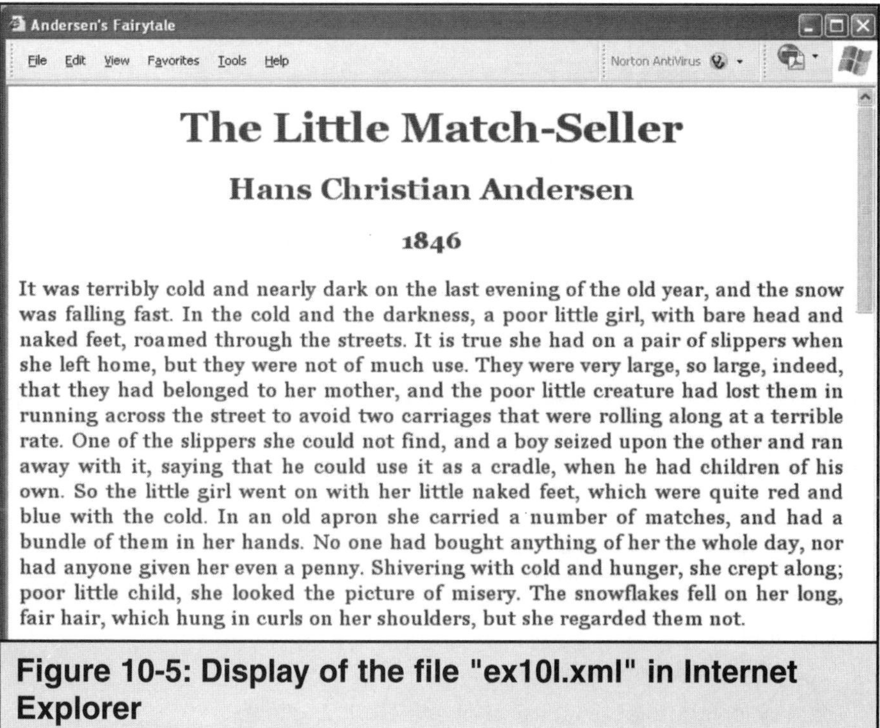

Figure 10-5: Display of the file "ex10I.xml" in Internet Explorer

The ft:paragraph element has mixed content: it can contain character data (i.e., text) interspersed with multiple occurrences of ft:speech elements. You can use this characteristic to further improve the display. For example, you can replace the template describing the ft:paragraph element’s pattern (Example

10-5, lines 23–25) with three discrete templates: one for the pattern ft:paragraph, one for the pattern ft:speech, and one for the pattern of character data (i.e., simple text content). Edit file "ex10H.xsl" to implement the above idea (see Example 10-6, lines 23–32). Save the file with the filename "ex10J.xsl."

Example 10-6: An XSLT style sheet with special output for the ft:speech element – filename: "ex10J.xsl"

```
1  <?xml version="1.0" encoding="UTF-8"?>
2  <xsl:stylesheet version="1.0"
3     xmlns:xsl="http://www.w3.org/1999/XSL/Transform"
4     xmlns:ft="http://justanexample.edu/fairytale/">
5     <xsl:template match="ft:fairytale">
6        <html>
7           <head><title>Andersen's Fairytale</title></head>
8              <body bgcolor="aliceblue">
9                 <font color="darkblue" face="Georgia, Arial">
10                   <xsl:apply-templates />
11                </font>
12             </body>
13       </html>
14    </xsl:template>
15    <xsl:template match="ft:metadata">
16       <xsl:apply-templates select="ft:descriptive"/>
17    </xsl:template>
18    <xsl:template match="ft:descriptive">
19       <h1 align="center"><xsl:value-of select="ft:title" /></h1>
20       <h2 align="center"><xsl:value-of select="ft:author" /></h2>
21       <h3 align="center"><xsl:value-of select="ft:year" /></h3>
22    </xsl:template>
23    <xsl:template match="ft:paragraph">
24       <p align="justify"> <xsl:apply-templates select="ft:speech | text()" /></p>
25    </xsl:template>
26    <xsl:template match="ft:speech">
27       <font color="purple"><xsl:value-of select="." /></font>
28    </xsl:template>
29    <xsl:template match="text()">
30       <xsl:value-of select="." />
31    </xsl:template>
32 </xsl:stylesheet>
```

In Example 10-6 (filename: "ex10J.xsl"), the template on line 23–25 specifies that whenever an XSLT processor sees an ft:paragraph element, it should apply the template with either an ft:speech element or with pure text as the matching pattern, depending on which child is encountered. The vertical pipe inside the value of the select attribute is a logical OR operator in the XPath language. The keyword text() represents a text node: in other words, it matches character data.

There are two other new templates in Example 10-6 (lines 26–31). Based on these two new templates, the content of the ft:speech element—the fairytale's dialogue—will be displayed in purple.

Modify the xml-stylesheet processing instructions in the file "ex10I.xml" to point to the XSLT stylesheet file "ex10J.xsl" instead "ex10H.xsl" and save the modified file as "ex10K.xml." You can also find the files in the accompanying CD under the Chapter10 folder. If you view the file "ex10K.xml" with an XSL compliant browser, you will see that all the dialogue is displayed in purple.

SERVER-SIDE XML PARSING

Up to now, all the instructions in this workbook assume that you are using not a specialized XML processor but a simple Web browser to parse XML documents. However, not all browsers can handle XSL transformations. In fact, as we see in Chapter 7, different Web browsers may process XML documents in slightly different ways. Therefore, you may want to parse the XML document on the server side and deliver the transformed HTML document in a way that is consistent for all clients.

If the syntax you use in the stylesheet file is not complicated, most modern Web browsers can transform XML documents to HTML documents on the client side without many problems. However, the source code of your XML files will be easily available to users; this may not always be desirable.

Transforming XML documents on the server side also allows you to apply different rules of transformation based on factors like the location, bandwidth, membership status, etc., of the client—even the very medium being used.

There are many ways to parse and transform an XML document on the server side. One of the easiest ways is to use PHP, a powerful scripting language for server-side programming. Using PHP, you don't need to worry about revealing your source code to ordinary viewers, as you will only be delivering the final results to the client.

Example 10-7 is a simple PHP script (filename: "ex10L.php") that transforms the source file "ex10K.xml" based on the XSLT stylesheet file "ex10J.xsl" and delivers the resulting HTML code back to the client. **To run this script, the files must be on a server, which should have the PHP XSLT extension installed, with the Sablotron library.**

If you don't have Sablotron library installed but you have PHP 5, you can use the following code, which will perform the same kind of operation:

```
<?php
   $dom = new domDocument();
   $dom->load("ex10J.xsl");
   $proc = new xsltprocessor;
   $xsl = $proc->importStylesheet($dom);
   $document = new domDocument();
   $document->load("ex10K.xml");
   print $proc->transformToXml($document);
?>
```

Example 10-7: A simple PHP script – filename: "ex10L.php"

```
1   <?php
2   $xml = "file://".getcwd()."/ex10K.xml";
3   $xsl = "file://".getcwd()."/ex10J.xsl";
4   $my_xslt = xslt_create();
5   $result = xslt_process($my_xslt,$xml,$xsl);
6   xslt_free($my_xslt);
7   print $result;
8   ?>
```

Example 10-7 assumes that the source XML document (i.e., "ex10K.xml"), the XSLT stylesheet file (i.e., "ex10J.xsl") and the PHP script (i.e., "ex10L.php") are all located in the same directory.

On line 2, the PHP program uses the command getcwd() to get the current working directory of the source XML document (i.e., "ex10K.xml") and assigns the filename with its path to a variable named $xml. On line 3, using the same approach, it assigns the filename and path information of the XSLT stylesheet file (i.e., "ex10J.xsl") to a variable named $xsl. On line 4, using the xslt_create() function, the program creates a new XSLT processor called $my_xslt. On line 5, the XSLT processor processes the source XML document with the corresponding XSLT style sheet and assigns the result (the transformed HTML document) to a variable named

$result. On line 6, the XSLT processor is destroyed to release its resources back to the computer. On line 7, the transformed HTML file is sent back to the browser.

When you use this PHP script for other XML source documents and XSLT stylesheet files, simply change the filenames on line 2 and line 3. Now, instead of giving out the locations of the source XML document and the XSLT stylesheet file, you give the URL of the PHP script. A user will get the transformed HTML document when the URL is activated and visited.

APPENDIX 1: MARC DTD — A SIMPLIFIED VERSION

This DTD is based on the official version of Bibliographic MARC DTD created by the Library of Congress. It was simplified to about 2% of the original for educational and pedagogical purposes.

In this DTD, a MARC record is divided into various container elements based on the eight areas of descriptions, main entry, and added entries prescribed by the *Anglo-American Cataloging Rules*, and on the traditional subject analysis and classification practices in the library world.

MARC fields and subfields are converted to XML elements with the corresponding MARC field numbers as part of the element names, e.g., the marcfield100 element for the MARC field 100; the marcfield245 element for the MARC field 245; and the marcfield245-a, marcfield245-b, and marcfield245-c elements for subfield a, subfield b, and subfield c of the MARC field 245, etc. MARC indicators are converted to attributes with the corresponding indicator number as part of the attributes. The first indicator is converted to the i1 attribute, and the second indicator is converted to i2 attribute.

The implementation is a very straightforward translation of the MARC standard, with explanation and meaning of most of the elements and attributes as comments. All of the techniques and syntaxes used in this DTD are very basic. It does not even use entity.

MARC DTD — A SIMPLIFIED VERSION. Based on the official Bibliographic MARC DTD created by Library of Congress. (Filename: "simple MARC.dtd".)

```
<?xml version="1.0" encoding="UTF-8"?>

<!ELEMENT marcrecord (marcfield-numbers-and-codes? , marcfield-main-entry? , marcfield-title-
and-title-related? , marcfield-edition-imprint-etc? , marcfield-physical-description? , marcfield-notes? ,
marcfield-subject-access?)>

<!ELEMENT marcfield-numbers-and-codes (marcfield050* , marcfield082*)>

<!ELEMENT marcfield050 ((marcfield050-a | marcfield050-b)*)>
<!ATTLIST marcfield050 name    CDATA   #FIXED "LIBRARY OF CONGRESS CALL NUMBER">
<!ATTLIST marcfield050 repeatable CDATA   #FIXED "yes">
```

(cont'd.)

MARC DTD — A SIMPLIFIED VERSION. Based on the official Bibliographic MARC DTD created by Library of Congress. (Filename: "simple MARC.dtd".) ***(Continued)***

```
<!-- Indicator1: Existence in LC collection -->
<!ATTLIST marcfield050 i1   (i1-blank | i1-0 | i1-1 )   #REQUIRED>
<!-- Indicator2: Source of call number -->
<!ATTLIST marcfield050 i2   (i2-blank | i2-0 | i2-4 )   #REQUIRED>

<!ELEMENT marcfield050-a (#PCDATA)>
<!ATTLIST marcfield050-a name   CDATA   #FIXED "Classification number">
<!ATTLIST marcfield050-a repeatable CDATA   #FIXED "yes">

<!ELEMENT marcfield050-b (#PCDATA)>
<!ATTLIST marcfield050-b name   CDATA   #FIXED "Item number">
<!ATTLIST marcfield050-b repeatable CDATA   #FIXED "no">

<!ELEMENT marcfield082 ((marcfield082-a | marcfield082-2)*)>
<!ATTLIST marcfield082 name   CDATA   #FIXED "DEWEY DECIMAL CALL NUMBER">
<!ATTLIST marcfield082 repeatable CDATA   #FIXED "yes">
<!-- Indicator1: Type of edition -->
<!ATTLIST marcfield082 i1   (i1-blank | i1-0 | i1-1 | i1-2 )   #REQUIRED>
<!-- Indicator2: Source of call number -->
<!ATTLIST marcfield082 i2   (i2-blank | i2-0 | i2-4 )   #REQUIRED>

<!ELEMENT marcfield082-a (#PCDATA)>
<!ATTLIST marcfield082-a name   CDATA   #FIXED "Classification number">
<!ATTLIST marcfield082-a repeatable CDATA   #FIXED "yes">

<!ELEMENT marcfield082-2 (#PCDATA)>
<!ATTLIST marcfield082-2 name   CDATA   #FIXED "Edition number">
<!ATTLIST marcfield082-2 repeatable CDATA   #FIXED "no">

<!ELEMENT marcfield-main-entry (marcfield100?)>

<!ELEMENT marcfield100 ((marcfield100-a | marcfield100-d | marcfield100-q)*)>
<!ATTLIST marcfield100 name   CDATA   #FIXED "MAIN ENTRY--PERSONAL NAME">
<!ATTLIST marcfield100 repeatable CDATA   #FIXED "no">
<!-- Indicator1: Type of personal name entry element -->
<!ATTLIST marcfield100 i1   (i1-0 | i1-1 | i1-3 )   #REQUIRED>
<!-- Indicator2: Undefined; contains a blank (#) -->
<!ATTLIST marcfield100 i2   (i2-blank )   "i2-blank">
```

(cont'd.)

MARC DTD — A SIMPLIFIED VERSION. Based on the official Bibliographic MARC DTD created by Library of Congress. (Filename: "simple MARC.dtd".) ***(Continued)***

```
<!ELEMENT marcfield100-a (#PCDATA)>
<!ATTLIST marcfield100-a name    CDATA    #FIXED "Personal name">
<!ATTLIST marcfield100-a repeatable CDATA    #FIXED "no">

<!ELEMENT marcfield100-d (#PCDATA)>
<!ATTLIST marcfield100-d name    CDATA    #FIXED "Dates associated with a name">
<!ATTLIST marcfield100-d repeatable CDATA    #FIXED "no">

<!ELEMENT marcfield100-q (#PCDATA)>
<!ATTLIST marcfield100-q name    CDATA    #FIXED "Fuller form of name">
<!ATTLIST marcfield100-q repeatable CDATA    #FIXED "no">

<!ELEMENT marcfield-title-and-title-related (marcfield245?)>

<!ELEMENT marcfield245 ((marcfield245-a | marcfield245-b | marcfield245-c)*)>
<!ATTLIST marcfield245 name    CDATA    #FIXED "TITLE STATEMENT">
<!ATTLIST marcfield245 repeatable CDATA    #FIXED "no">
<!-- Indicator1: Title added entry -->
<!ATTLIST marcfield245 i1    (i1-0 | i1-1 )    #REQUIRED>
<!-- Indicator2: Nonfiling characters -->
<!ATTLIST marcfield245 i2    (i2-0 |
        i2-1 |
        i2-2 |
        i2-3 |
        i2-4 |
        i2-5 |
        i2-6 |
        i2-7 |
        i2-8 |
        i2-9 )    #REQUIRED>

<!ELEMENT marcfield245-a (#PCDATA)>
<!ATTLIST marcfield245-a name    CDATA    #FIXED "Title">
<!ATTLIST marcfield245-a repeatable CDATA    #FIXED "no">

<!ELEMENT marcfield245-b (#PCDATA)>
<!ATTLIST marcfield245-b name    CDATA    #FIXED "Remainder of title">
<!ATTLIST marcfield245-b repeatable CDATA    #FIXED "no">
```

(cont'd.)

MARC DTD — A SIMPLIFIED VERSION. Based on the official Bibliographic MARC DTD created by Library of Congress. (Filename: "simple MARC.dtd".) ***(Continued)***

```
<!ELEMENT marcfield245-c (#PCDATA)>
<!ATTLIST marcfield245-c name   CDATA   #FIXED "Remainder of title page transcription/statement
of responsibility">
<!ATTLIST marcfield245-c repeatable CDATA   #FIXED "no">

<!ELEMENT marcfield-edition-imprint-etc (marcfield250? , marcfield260?)>

<!ELEMENT marcfield250 ((marcfield250-a | marcfield250-b)*)>
<!ATTLIST marcfield250 name   CDATA   #FIXED "EDITION STATEMENT">
<!ATTLIST marcfield250 repeatable CDATA   #FIXED "no">
<!-- Indicator1: Undefined; contains a blank (#) -->
<!ATTLIST marcfield250 i1   (i1-blank )   "i1-blank">
<!-- Indicator2: Undefined; contains a blank (#) -->
<!ATTLIST marcfield250 i2   (i2-blank )   "i2-blank">

<!ELEMENT marcfield250-a (#PCDATA)>
<!ATTLIST marcfield250-a name   CDATA   #FIXED "Edition statement">
<!ATTLIST marcfield250-a repeatable CDATA   #FIXED "no">

<!ELEMENT marcfield250-b (#PCDATA)>
<!ATTLIST marcfield250-b name   CDATA   #FIXED "Remainder of edition statement">
<!ATTLIST marcfield250-b repeatable CDATA   #FIXED "no">

<!ELEMENT marcfield260 ((marcfield260-a | marcfield260-b | marcfield260-c)*)>
<!ATTLIST marcfield260 name   CDATA   #FIXED "PUBLICATION, DISTRIBUTION, ETC.
(IMPRINT)">
<!ATTLIST marcfield260 repeatable CDATA #FIXED "no">
<!-- Indicator1: Sequence of publishing statements -->
<!ATTLIST marcfield260 i1   (i1-blank | i1-2 | i1-3)   #REQUIRED>
<!-- Indicator2: Undefined; contains a blank (#) -->
<!ATTLIST marcfield260 i2   (i2-blank )   "i2-blank">

<!ELEMENT marcfield260-a (#PCDATA)>
<!ATTLIST marcfield260-a name   CDATA   #FIXED "Place of publication, distribution, etc.">
<!ATTLIST marcfield260-a repeatable CDATA   #FIXED "yes">

<!ELEMENT marcfield260-b (#PCDATA)>
<!ATTLIST marcfield260-b name   CDATA   #FIXED "Name of publisher, distributor, etc.">
<!ATTLIST marcfield260-b repeatable CDATA   #FIXED "yes">
```

(cont'd.)

MARC DTD — A SIMPLIFIED VERSION. Based on the official Bibliographic MARC DTD created by Library of Congress. (Filename: "simple MARC.dtd".) ***(Continued)***

```
<!ELEMENT marcfield260-c (#PCDATA)>
<!ATTLIST marcfield260-c name   CDATA   #FIXED "Date of publication, distribution, etc.">
<!ATTLIST marcfield260-c repeatable CDATA   #FIXED "yes">

<!ELEMENT marcfield-physical-description (marcfield300*)>

<!ELEMENT marcfield300 ((marcfield300-a | marcfield300-b | marcfield300-c | marcfield300-e)*)>
<!ATTLIST marcfield300 name   CDATA   #FIXED "PHYSICAL DESCRIPTION">
<!ATTLIST marcfield300 repeatable CDATA   #FIXED "yes">
<!-- Indicator1: Undefined; contains a blank (#) -->
<!ATTLIST marcfield300 i1   (i1-blank )   "i1-blank">
<!-- Indicator2: Undefined; contains a blank (#) -->
<!ATTLIST marcfield300 i2   (i2-blank )   "i2-blank">

<!ELEMENT marcfield300-a (#PCDATA)>
<!ATTLIST marcfield300-a name   CDATA   #FIXED "Extent">
<!ATTLIST marcfield300-a repeatable CDATA   #FIXED "yes">

<!ELEMENT marcfield300-b (#PCDATA)>
<!ATTLIST marcfield300-b name   CDATA   #FIXED "Other physical details">
<!ATTLIST marcfield300-b repeatable CDATA   #FIXED "no">

<!ELEMENT marcfield300-c (#PCDATA)>
<!ATTLIST marcfield300-c name   CDATA   #FIXED "Dimensions">
<!ATTLIST marcfield300-c repeatable CDATA   #FIXED "yes">

<!ELEMENT marcfield300-e (#PCDATA)>
<!ATTLIST marcfield300-e name   CDATA   #FIXED "Accompanying material">
<!ATTLIST marcfield300-e repeatable CDATA   #FIXED "no">

<!ELEMENT marcfield-notes (marcfield500*)>

<!ELEMENT marcfield500 (marcfield500-a*)>
<!ATTLIST marcfield500 name   CDATA   #FIXED "GENERAL NOTE">
<!ATTLIST marcfield500 repeatable CDATA   #FIXED "yes">
<!-- Indicator1: Undefined; contains a blank (#) -->
<!ATTLIST marcfield500 i1   (i1-blank )   "i1-blank">
<!-- Indicator2: Undefined; contains a blank (#) -->
<!ATTLIST marcfield500 i2   (i2-blank )   "i2-blank">
```

(cont'd.)

MARC DTD — A SIMPLIFIED VERSION. Based on the official Bibliographic MARC DTD created by Library of Congress. (Filename: "simple MARC.dtd".) ***(Continued)***

```
<!ELEMENT marcfield500-a (#PCDATA)>
<!ATTLIST marcfield500-a name   CDATA   #FIXED "General note">
<!ATTLIST marcfield500-a repeatable CDATA   #FIXED "no">

<!ELEMENT marcfield-subject-access (marcfield650*)>

<!ELEMENT marcfield650 ((marcfield650-a | marcfield650-b | marcfield650-v | marcfield650-x |
marcfield650-y | marcfield650-z)*)>
<!ATTLIST marcfield650 name   CDATA   #FIXED "SUBJECT ADDED ENTRY--TOPICAL TERM">
<!ATTLIST marcfield650 repeatable CDATA   #FIXED "yes">
<!-- Indicator1: Level of subject -->
<!ATTLIST marcfield650 i1   (i1-blank | i1-0 | i1-1 | i1-2 )   #REQUIRED>
<!-- Indicator2: Subject heading system/thesaurus -->
<!ATTLIST marcfield650 i2   (i2-0 |
        i2-1 |
        i2-2 |
        i2-3 |
        i2-4 |
        i2-5 |
        i2-6 |
        2-7 )   #REQUIRED>

<!ELEMENT marcfield650-a (#PCDATA)>
<!ATTLIST marcfield650-a name   CDATA   #FIXED "Topical term or geographic name as entry
element (NR)">
<!ATTLIST marcfield650-a repeatable CDATA   #FIXED "yes">

<!ELEMENT marcfield650-b (#PCDATA)>
<!ATTLIST marcfield650-b name   CDATA   #FIXED "Topical term following geographic name as
entry element">
<!ATTLIST marcfield650-b repeatable CDATA   #FIXED "no">

<!ELEMENT marcfield650-v (#PCDATA)>
<!ATTLIST marcfield650-v name   CDATA   #FIXED "Form subdivision">
<!ATTLIST marcfield650-v repeatable CDATA   #FIXED "yes">

<!ELEMENT marcfield650-x (#PCDATA)>
<!ATTLIST marcfield650-x name   CDATA   #FIXED "General subdivision">
<!ATTLIST marcfield650-x repeatable CDATA   #FIXED "yes">
```

(cont'd.)

MARC DTD — A SIMPLIFIED VERSION. Based on the official Bibliographic MARC DTD created by Library of Congress. (Filename: "simple MARC.dtd".) ***(Continued)***

```
<!ELEMENT marcfield650-y (#PCDATA)>
<!ATTLIST marcfield650-y name    CDATA    #FIXED "Chronological subdivision">
<!ATTLIST marcfield650-y repeatable CDATA    #FIXED "yes">

<!ELEMENT marcfield650-z (#PCDATA)>
<!ATTLIST marcfield650-z name    CDATA    #FIXED "Geographic subdivision">
<!ATTLIST marcfield650-z repeatable CDATA    #FIXED "yes">
```

2 APPENDIX 2: THE MARC21 SLIM SCHEMA

After the development of the DTDs for Bibliographic MARC and Authority MARC, the Library of Congress developed a flexible and extensible schema for MARC, implemented in the W3C XML Schema Language. It is called MARC21 SLIM. It can be used to represent a complete MARC record in XML. MARC DTDs support only two MARC formats (i.e., Bibliographic MARC, Authority MARC). The MARC21 SLIM Schema supports all five of the MARC formats (Bibliographic MARC, Authority MARC, Holdings MARC, Classification MARC, and Community Information MARC). You may be surprised to learn that, instead of thousands of lines of code like the two MARC DTDs, MARC21 SLIM Schema consists of fewer than 150 lines of code, documentation included. The only limitation is, you need to use an external software to enforce its validation.

For beginners, the MARC21 SLIM Schema is not easy to understand, even the names of the element types, attributes, and data types declared and defined in the schema may be confusing enough to stop one from reading. For example, in the schema, it declares an element type named record, which has a recordType type. In addition, a record element in an instance document may have a type attribute, which has a recordTypeType type, and so forth. These names are the official vocabularies from the original MARC21 SLIM Schema, not my creation to confuse you. However, once you get used to this naming convention, they will become helpful hints for the creation of instance documents of catalog records. After you have finished reading all of the fragments, read the complete version at the end of this appendix.

Just like the MARC DTD, the MARC21 SLIM Schema retains the semantics of MARC. MARC fields are treated as elements, and MARC indicators are directly converted to attributes. MARC subfields are directly converted to child elements, with the subfield code as an attribute. In the following examples, we will break the schema into multiple sequential fragments for discussion and reassemble them at the end of the appendix.

1. THE XML DECLARATION AND THE ROOT ELEMENT OF THE SCHEMA

Fragment 1: The XML Declaration and the Root Element

```
1   <?xml version="1.0" encoding="UTF-8"?>
2   <xsd:schema
3       xmlns="http://www.loc.gov/MARC21/slim"
4       xmlns:xsd="http://www.w3.org/2001/XMLSchema"
5       targetNamespace="http://www.loc.gov/MARC21/slim"
6       elementFormDefault="qualified"
7   >
8   ... ...
9   ... ...
10  </xsd:schema>
```

Fragment 1 is the XML declaration and the root element of the schema. The root element is xsd:schema (line 2), which is the root element for all W3C XML schema files. There are two namespace declaration attributes inside the start-tag of the root element. The first (line 3) is a default namespace declaration for the MARC21 SLIM Schema. All elements and attributes that have no prefixes will belong to this namespace. The second namespace declaration (line 4) associates the xsd prefix with the namespace URI of the W3C XML Schema Language.

Line 5 is the targetNamespace attribute, which spells out the namespace URI of all the vocabularies created by this schema. Its value will be used by an XML processor to match with the namespace URI used in instance documents. As you can see, the value here is identical to the default namespace of the schema (i.e., both are "http://www.loc.gov/MARC21/slim"). However, an XML parser will not know anything about this. It will only use the value of the targetNamespace attribute for matching.

The elementFormDefault attribute on line 6 is to specify that in an instance document child elements must have prefixes to identify their namespaces. In other words, you should not use the shorthand format, in which, when a parent element already has a namespace prefix, you may omit the prefixes for the child elements. The elementFormDefault attribute is one of the two attributes that you can use to specify whether you want the local element and attributes in an instance document to use prefixes or not. The other attribute is the attributeFormDefault attribute. Both of them have "unqualified" as their default value, so you don't need to include the attributes if you are not going to change the default value.

2. THE RECORD ELEMENT TYPE

Fragment 2: The element type declaration of record

```
1   … …
2   <xsd:element name="record" type="recordType" nillable="true" id="record.e">
3       <xsd:annotation>
4           <xsd:documentation> record is a top level container element for all of
5           the field elements which compose the record </xsd:documentation>
6       </xsd:annotation>
7   </xsd:element>
8   … …
```

Fragment 2 is the first child element of the xsd:schema element. It is an element type declaration. The name of the element type is record. There is a nillable attribute in the start-tag of the element element (line 2), the value of which equals "true". Based on this, an instance document may have the xsi:nil="true" attribute inside a record element, e.g., <record xsi:nil="true"> </record>.

In an instance document, when there is the xsi:nil="true" attribute inside the start-tag of an element, that element should be accepted as valid when it has no content, whether its content type allows empty content or not. The nil attribute is defined as part of the XML Schema Namespace for Instances, so it must appear in the instance document with a prefix (such as xsi) associated with the namespace: http://www.w3.org/2001/XMLSchema-instance. The nil mechanism applies only to element values, not to attribute values. An element with the xsi:nil="true" attribute must be empty but it may still carry attributes.

The record element has a data type called recordType (line 2). Since this type is not defined in this block of code, it must be defined later as a global type somewhere in the schema.

Under the xsd:element element, there is an annotation element (line 4) from the xsd namespace. The annotation element is used for storing comments for humans to read or instruction for applications to process. If it has comments for the human reader, the comments will be stored in the documentation child element; if it has instructions for an application to process, the instruction will be stored in the appinfo child element. There are many places in a schema to insert an annotation element, for instance, as the first child of an element element, or as the first child of a type definition, etc.

3. THE COLLECTION ELEMENT TYPE

Fragment 3: The element type declaration of collection

```
... ...
<xsd:element name="collection" type="collectionType"
      nillable="true" id="collection.e">
   <xsd:annotation>
      <xsd:documentation> collection is a top level container element for 0 or
         many records </xsd:documentation>
   </xsd:annotation>
</xsd:element>
... ...
```

Fragment 3 is the second element type declaration in the schema. This is an element declaration for collection, which has a data type named collectionType.

This is the second global element declared in this schema. The first global element declared is record. Accordingly, an instance element can use either the record element or the collection element as its root element. In other words, this schema is good for creating just one catalog record (i.e., with record as its root element), and it is also good for creating a collection of records (i.e., with collection as its root element.) Based on this understanding, in the definition of the collectionType data type, you should expect to see the record element there, as a child element inside the type definition of the collectionType type.

4. THE DEFINITION OF THE COLLECTIONTYPE TYPE

Fragment 4: The definition of the of the collectionType type

```
1   ... ...
2   <xsd:complexType name="collectionType" id="collection.ct">
3       <xsd:sequence minOccurs="0" maxOccurs="unbounded">
4           <xsd:element ref="record"/>
5       </xsd:sequence>
6       <xsd:attribute name="id" type="idDataType" use="optional"/>
7   </xsd:complexType>
8   ... ...
```

Fragment 4 is the first type definition in the schema. The type is given a name (i.e., collectionType). Only when a type has a name can it be used by reference in the schema, as used in Fragment 3, line 2. Using the complexType element from the xsd namespace, Fragment 4 defines the structure of a complex data type named collectionType. As a complex type, it can contain child elements and attributes. Based on the code from line 3 to line 5, an element that has this type (e.g., the collection element) can have 0 (minOccurs="0") to unlimited (maxOccurs="unbounded") number of record elements as its child elements.

There is a local attribute declaration on line 6. It is local because the declaration is not a child of the xsd:schema element, but a child of the complexType element. In other words, the attribute can only be an attribute of an element when its type attribute equals collectionType. Based on the code, in an instance document, an element that has collectionType as its type can have an attribute named id, but its presence is optional (use="optional"). It is OK to omit the id attribute.

Since there is already an element type declaration for record, it cannot be re-declared. Instead, the ref attribute is used on line 4.

In an instance document, if you combine the codes in Fragments 3 and 4, you can have a collection element as a root element, which can contain multiple record elements, like a database of catalog records. However, up to this point, it is still not clear what a record element should look like because its data type (i.e., recordType, see Fragment 2, line 2) has not yet been defined. Its definition is in the next fragment of code.

5. DEFINITION OF THE RECORDTYPE TYPE

Fragment 5: The definition of the recordType type

```
1    ... ...
2    <xsd:complexType name="recordType" id="record.ct">
3        <xsd:sequence minOccurs="0">
4            <xsd:element name="leader" type="leaderFieldType"/>
5            <xsd:element name="controlfield" type="controlFieldType"
6                    minOccurs="0" maxOccurs="unbounded"/>
7            <xsd:element name="datafield" type="dataFieldType"
8                    minOccurs="0" maxOccurs="unbounded"/>
9        </xsd:sequence>
10       <xsd:attribute name="type" type="recordTypeType" use="optional"/>
11       <xsd:attribute name=“id” type=“idDataType” use=“optional”/>
12   </xsd:complexType>
13   ... ...
```

This is the type definition for the recordType type; the record declared in Fragment 2 has this data type. According to this definition, a record element should contain exactly one leader element (line 4), followed by zero or more controlfield elements (line 5), followed by zero or more datafield elements (line 7). The sequential order of these three child elements cannot be changed in an instance document. Accordingly, in an instance document, a record element will look like this:

```
<record ... ... >
    <leader>      ... ... </leader>
    <controlField> ... ... </controlField>
    <dataField> ... ... </dataField>
</record>
```

Obviously the leader element, the controlfield element, and the datafield element are corresponding to the leader, the variable control fields, and the variable data fields of the general MARC record structure. Therefore, you can expect to see later in the definitions of the leaderType, controlFieldType, and dataFieldType types that they will be exactly parallel to the MARC leader (the first 24 digits of a MARC record), MARC variable control fields (the MARC number begins with double 0), and MARC variable data fields (other MARC numbers).

There are two local attribute declarations on lines 10 and 11; both with use="optional". Therefore, a record element in an instance document can have two optional attributes. They are the type attribute and the id attribute. There are five different MARC record formats; the type attribute will be used to specify which MARC format the record belongs to. The data type of the type attribute (i.e., recordTypeType) is defined in the next block of code.

6. THE RECORDTYPETYPE TYPE FOR MARC FORMAT

Fragment 6: The definition of the data type of the type attribute of a record element

```
... ...
<xsd:simpleType name="recordTypeType" id="type.st">
    <xsd:restriction base="xsd:NMTOKEN">
        <xsd:enumeration value="Bibliographic"/>
        <xsd:enumeration value="Authority"/>
        <xsd:enumeration value="Holdings"/>
        <xsd:enumeration value="Classification"/>
        <xsd:enumeration value="Community"/>
    </xsd:restriction>
</xsd:simpleType>
... ...
```

Fragment 6 is a type definition for the recordTypeType. Let's trace back the code to see where we need to use this recordTypeType. Based on Fragments 2 and 5, an instance document can have a record element like this:

```
<record type="...  ..." id="...  ..." >
    <leader>      ... ... </leader>
    <controlField> ... ... </controlField>
    <dataField> ... ... </dataField>
</record>
```

Inside the start-tag of the record element, there is a type attribute. The type attribute has a special data type: recordTypeType (Fragment 5, line 10). Fragment 6 defines the value of this type attribute. Now let's examine the definition of the recordTypeType type.

The type definition is inside the xsd:simpleType element (Fragment 6, line 2). Just like the complexType element is used to define new data type, the simpleType element is also used to define new data type. However the data type that the simpleType element defines cannot have child elements, nor can it have any attributes. Since what is going to be defined will be used as the data type of the value of an attribute (i.e., the type attribute of the record element), a child element is of course out of the question, and the attribute value cannot have an attribute. Hence, the simpleType element should be used.

This is a type definition by derivation. In Chapter 9, you learned how to derive a new data type from an existing data type using the xsd:extension element. When you use the xsd:extension element, you add more elements and attributes to the base type to derive new types. There is another way to derive a new data type from an existing data type, that is to use the xsd:restriction element, as shown here in Fragment 6, line 3.

When you use the xsd:restriction element, you impose more constraints on the base type to derive a new type. The base type specified here is NMTOKEN. It means any mixture of XML Name characters. Basically, it is a combination of characters, numbers, and a few other punctuation marks, with certain constraints. (Reread Chapter 3 if you have forgotten what an XML Name is.) Now the derived data type is more restrictive than NMTOKEN.

Inside the xsd:restriction element, there are multiple xsd:enumeration elements. The xsd:enumeration elements are used to list all of the allowed values using the value attributes. There are five xsd:enumeration elements with five value attributes (i.e., Bibliographic, Authority, Holdings, Classification, and Community). The consequence of this specification for an instance document is that the type attribute of a record element can only take Bibliographic, Authority, Holdings, Classification, or Community as its value. These five values are exactly the same as the names of the five different MARC formats. Clearly this is used for identifying the MARC format of the record. For instance, if the XML document is a bibliographic MARC record, then we will have the following:

```
<record type="Bibliograpic" id="... ..." >
   <leaderField>        ... ... </leadField>
   <controlField> ... ... </controlField>
   <dataField> ... ... </dataField>
</record>
```

7. MARC LEADER

The MARC leader consists of the first 24 digits (position 0 to position 23) of a MARC record and provides information for the automatic processing of the record. It consists of data elements that contain coded values. The meaning of the data elements are identified by relative character position. Now, see how the MARC21 SLIM schema handles the MARC leader.

Fragment 7: The definitions of leaderFieldType and leadDataType

```
... ...
<xsd:complexType name="leaderFieldType" id="leader.ct">
   <xsd:annotation>
      <xsd:documentation>MARC21 Leader, 24 bytes</xsd:documentation>
   </xsd:annotation>
   <xsd:simpleContent>
      <xsd:extension base="leaderDataType">
         <xsd:attribute name="id" type="idDataType" use="optional"/>
      </xsd:extension>
   </xsd:simpleContent>
</xsd:complexType>

<xsd:simpleType name="leaderDataType" id="leader.st">
   <xsd:restriction base="xsd:string">
      <xsd:whiteSpace value="preserve"/>
      <xsd:pattern
         value="[\d ]{5}[\dA-Za-z ]{1}[\dA-Za-z]{1}[\dA-Za-z ]{3}(2|  )(2|  )
                [\d ] {5}[\dA-Za-z ]{3}(4500|    )" />
   </xsd:restriction>
</xsd:simpleType>
... ...
```

To store the data of a MARC leader, the schema declares an element type named leader in Fragment 5, line 4: <xsd:element name="leader" type="leaderFieldType"/>. It means that the leader has a data type called leaderFieldType, which is derived from a data type called leaderDataType. Fragment 7 has the definitions of the leadFieldType and leaderDataType.

In Fragment 7, the first child of the complexType element is the annotation element (line 2). The comment inside the documentation element of the annotation element is from the official schema, not the words of the author of this book. It states that the data type to be defined in this definition is for storing the 24 digits of a MARC leader.

When you use the complexType element to derive a new data type based on an existing data type, you can specify whether the new type will have simple content (i.e., no child element) or complex content (i.e., child elements). Fragment 7 uses the simpleContent child element (line 6) so the derived data type cannot have any child element, but it has an optional attribute (line 8).

The new type is based on an existing data type called leaderDataType. It is created by using the extension element to add an attribute (lines 7 to 9) to the base type. The base type, leaderDataType, is not a built-in data type, so it must be defined somewhere in the schema. In addition, since the new type will have simple content and the derivation method is extension, not restriction, the base type must also have simple content. The base type, leaderDataType, is defined from line 13 to line 20.

The leaderDataType is itself also a type derived from an existing type. The base type is string, and the derivation method is restriction (line 14). Therefore, you should expect this data type to have only some special characters or numbers.

On line 15, inside the xsd:restriction element, there is a xsd:whiteSpace element with value equals to "preserve". The xsd:whiteSpace element is used to specify whether white spaces should be collapsed or not. In many examples in this book, the use of white spaces is only for easier reading and they don't have special meaning, so we don't need to preserve white space. In a MARC leader, there must be 24 digits, but some of the digits can be empty spaces. When a digit is an empty space, it has special meaning. Therefore, in the specification of what the 24 digits can be, white space should be preserved. Let's examine closely how the 24 digits of the MARC leader are specified (lines 16 to 18):

```
<xsd:pattern
   value="[\d ]{5}[\dA-Za-z ]{1}[\dA-Za-z]{1}[\dA-Za-z ]{3}(2|  )(2|  )
         [\d ]{5}[\dA-Za-z ]{3}(4500|    )"/>
```

First of all, it uses the pattern element for the specification. The pattern element is usually used in conjunction with a regular expression to express a pattern. The regular expression is in the value attribute. Its syntax is similar to the regular expression syntax of other programming languages. Here are the rules:

- \d This means a numeric digit
- [\d] This means there is one digit, which can be a single digit numeral, or an empty space. (Square bracket

means options set. All options included in the square bracket are legal candidates for selection.)

- [\dA-Za-z] This means a numeric digit, a letter, or an empty space.
- [\dA-Za-z]{n} This means that a numeric digit, a letter, or an empty space appears n times. (A number inside curly braces indicates number of occurrences.)
- (x|y) This means x or y. (Vertical bar represents logical "or.")

Now we can decode the value attribute of the xsd:pattern element.

- [\d]{5} This means five numeric digits or empty spaces. It corresponds to the first five positions of a MARC leader, which make up a five-character numeric string that specifies the length of the entire record. Each unused position contains a zero.
- [\dA-Za-z]{1} This means one numeric digit or one letter. It corresponds to the sixth position of a MARC leader, which indicates the relation of the record to a file (e.g., the letter **a** in this position indicates that the encoding level of the record has been changed to a higher encoding level, the letter **c** indicates a change other than in the encoding level code has been made to the record, etc.)
- [\dA-Za-z]{1} This pattern has the same meaning as the pattern immediately above. It corresponds to the seventh position of a MARC leader, which indicates the characteristics of the record (e.g., the letter **c** in this position represents notated music, the letter **e** represents cartographic material, the letter **k** represents two-dimensional nonprojectable graphic, etc.)
- [\dA-Za-z]{3} The pattern has the same meaning as the two preceding patterns, but it can appear three times. It represents the eighth, ninth, and tenth positions of a MARC leader, which indicate the bibliographic level, type of control, and the character-coding scheme.
- (2|) This means either a number 2 or an empty space. It corresponds to the 11th position of a MARC leader, which indicates the number of character positions used for indicators in a variable data field.
- (2|) The pattern has the same meaning as above. It corresponds to the 12th position of a MARC leader, which indicates the number of character positions used for each subfield code in a variable data field.

- [\d]{5} This means five numeric digits. It corresponds to the 13th to 17th positions of a MARC leader, which is the base address of the data. It consists of a five-character numeric string that indicates the first character position of the first variable control field in a record. Unused positions contain a zero.
- [\dA-Za-z]{3} This pattern has appeared in this list a few times already. It corresponds to the 18th to 20th positions of a MARC leader. They indicate encoding level, descriptive catalog form, and linked record requirements.
- (4500|) This means either the number 4,500 or four empty spaces. It corresponds to the last four positions of a MARC leader. They indicate the structure of each entry in the directory and must be 4500. Four empty spaces means undefined.

8. THE VARIABLE CONTROL FIELD

The variable control fields of MARC records are the fields with double zero and a single numeral as their field numbers (e.g., in Bibliographic MARC, they are 001, 003, 005, 006, 007, and 008). They contain control information that is used in processing the MARC records. Unlike data variable fields, control variable fields do not have indicators.

The MARC21 SLIM Schema uses the controlField element (see Fragment 5, line 5) to store the data of control variable fields. Fragment 8 is the definition of the type that the controlField element has: controlFieldType. Basically, it uses the same implementation approach as the MARC leader. That is, it defines a type and uses it as a container for all the information that is supposed to be included. If some of the information to be included is too complicated, it creates a new type to handle it separately, and then uses the new type as the base type for the container.

Fragment 8: The definition of controlFieldType and its base type

```
… …
<xsd:complexType name="controlFieldType" id="controlfield.ct">
  <xsd:annotation>
    <xsd:documentation>MARC21 Fields 001-009</xsd:documentation>
```

(cont'd.)

Fragment 8: The definition of controlFieldType and its base type *(Continued)*

```
5     </xsd:annotation>
6     <xsd:simpleContent>
7        <xsd:extension base="controlDataType">
8           <xsd:attribute name="id" type="idDataType" use="optional"/>
9           <xsd:attribute name="tag" type="controltagDataType" use="required"/>
10       </xsd:extension>
11    </xsd:simpleContent>
12 </xsd:complexType>
13
14 <xsd:simpleType name="controlDataType" id="controlfield.st">
15    <xsd:restriction base="xsd:string">
16       <xsd:whiteSpace value="preserve"/>
17    </xsd:restriction>
18 </xsd:simpleType>
19
20 <xsd:simpleType name="controltagDataType" id="controltag.st">
21    <xsd:restriction base="xsd:string">
22       <xsd:whiteSpace value="preserve"/>
23       <xsd:pattern value="00[1-9A-Za-z]{1}"/>
24    </xsd:restriction>
25 </xsd:simpleType>
26 ... ...
```

In Fragment 8, the first block of codes (line 2–line 12) works like a container. It uses the complexType element to derive a new type called controlFieldType type based on an existing type called controlDataType type (line 7). Two attributes are added (lines 8 and 9) to the base type, they are id and tag. Based on Fragment 5, line 5, and this block of code, in an instance document you can have

```
<controlField tag="..... " id="... ..." >
... ...
</controlField>
```

The tag attribute in the above few lines of code has the data type named controltagDataType (see Fragment 8, line 9); the definition for this data type is in the third block of codes in Fragment 8 (lines 20–25). It is a simple type derived from a primitive type xsd:string using the restriction method (lines 21 and 24). There are two specifications in the derivation:

```
<xsd:whiteSpace value="preserve"/>
<xsd:pattern value="00[1-9A-Za-z]{1}"/>
```

You should now be able to understand the pattern in the above code. It means that the value must be three digits, starting with 2 zeros and ending with either a number or a letter. Accordingly, in the instance document, you can have <controlField tag="001" id="... ..." > ... ... </controlField> to represent control data field 001, or, <controlField tag="006" id="... ..." > ... ... </controlField> to represent control data field 006, etc.

The base type of the controlFieldType type is the controlDataType type; the definition for this in the second block of codes in Fragment 8, (lines 14–18). Basically, it specifies that the content of the controlField element is character data or text string, with meaningful empty spaces so you can put in almost anything.

9. THE VARIABLE DATA FIELD

The variable data fields of MARC records are the fields not beginning with double zero. They contain the content of a MARC record. Within each variable data field, there are two indicators and various subfields. The MARC 21SLIM schema uses the dataField element (see Fragment 5, line 7) to store the data of these fields. The dataField element has a type called dataFieldType. Its definition is in Fragment 9.

Fragment 9: The definition of dataFieldType

```
... ...
<xsd:complexType name="dataFieldType" id="datafield.ct">
    <xsd:annotation>
        <xsd:documentation>MARC21 Variable Data Fields 010-999</xsd:documentation>
    </xsd:annotation>
    <xsd:sequence maxOccurs="unbounded">
        <xsd:element name="subfield" type="subfieldatafieldType"/>
    </xsd:sequence>
    <xsd:attribute name="id" type="idDataType" use="optional"/>
    <xsd:attribute name="tag" type="tagDataType" use="required"/>
    <xsd:attribute name="ind1" type="indicatorDataType" use="required"/>
    <xsd:attribute name="ind2" type="indicatorDataType" use="required"/>
</xsd:complexType>
... ...
```

Fragment 9 is a complex-type definition for the dataFieldType type. As specified in the documentation element (line 4), this data type is for storing "MARC21 Variable Data Fields 010-999". In this definition, there is only one element type declaration (line 7), which declares an element type called subfield. The element type declaration is a child element of a sequence element that has a maxOccurrs attribute with value equals to "unbounded" (line 6). Based on Fragment 9, lines 6–8 and Fragment 5, line 7, in an instance document you can have:

```
<dataField ... ...>
    <subfield ... ...> ... ... </subfield>
    ... ...
    <subfield ... ...>... ... </subfield>
</dataField>
```

There are four attribute declarations (lines 9–12). Three of them must be present. They are tag, ind1, and ind2. Therefore, in an instance document, you now can have:

```
<dataField tag="..." ind1="..." ind2="..." >
    <subfield ... ...> ... ... </subfield>
    ... ...
    <subfield ... ...>... ... </subfield>
</dataField>
```

The data type of the tag attribute is the tagDataType (Fragment 9, line 11). The data type of both the ind1 attribute and the ind2 attribute is the indicatorDataType type (Fragment 9, lines 11–12). Their definitions are in Fragment 10.

Fragment 10: The definition of tagDataType type and indicatorDataType

```
... ...
<xsd:simpleType name="tagDataType" id="tag.st">
    <xsd:restriction base="xsd:string">
        <xsd:whiteSpace value="preserve"/>
        <xsd:pattern value="(0([1-9A-Z][0-9A-Z])|0([1-9a-z][0-9a-z]))|
(([1-9A-Z][0-9A-Z]{2})|([1-9a-z][0-9a-z]{2}))"/>
    </xsd:restriction>
</xsd:simpleType>

```

(cont'd.)

Fragment 10: The definition of tagDataType type and indicatorDataType *(Continued)*

```
10    <xsd:simpleType name="indicatorDataType" id="ind.st">
11        <xsd:restriction base="xsd:string">
12            <xsd:whiteSpace value="preserve"/>
13            <xsd:pattern value="[\da-z ]{1}"/>
14        </xsd:restriction>
15    </xsd:simpleType>
16    ... ...
```

The definition of tagDataType is in the first block of Fragment 10 (lines 2–8). The allowed values of this type are expressed in regular expression (lines 5–6), which basically means that there are three alphanumeric digits; if the first digit is 0, then the second digit cannot be 0. This type is clearly for the MARC variable data field. Note that although legally letters may be used in the 3 digits (e.g., "123"), up until now, no letter (e.g., "xyz") has ever been assigned. The legal and defined MARC variable data fields still consist only of three numeric digits, no alphabet yet.

The definition of the indicatorDataField is in the second block of code in Fragment 10 (lines 10–14). It is also expressed in regular expression, which basically means the value can be either a single numeric digit, a letter, or an empty space. This type is for the value of the two indicators of a MARC record. Once again, although a letter is a legal candidate to be used as an indicator value, it has never been used.

Based on Fragments 9 and 10, in an instance document, you now can have the following or any other similar MARC field.

```
<dataField tag="245" ind1="1" ind2="4">
    <subfield ... ...>The little match-seller </subfield>
    <subfield ... ...>Hans Christian Andersen</subfield>
</dataField>
```

As specified in Fragment 9, line 7, the subfield element has a data type called subfielddatafieldType, which, in fact, is a complex type derived from an existing type called subfieldDataType and uses the extension element (see Fragment 11, line 4). The extension adds two attributes to the base type (Fragment 11, lines 5–8). One attribute is optional, and the other attribute is required. The required attribute has a data type called subfieldcodeDataType. Basically, these three types (subfielddatafieldType, subfieldDataType, and subfieldcodeDataType) determine the structure of a subfield. Fragment 11 shows the definitions of these three types

Fragment 11: The definitions of subfieldatafieldType, subfieldDataType and subfieldcodeDataType

```
1   … …
2   <xsd:complexType name="subfieldatafieldType" id="subfield.ct">
3       <xsd:simpleContent>
4           <xsd:extension base="subfieldDataType">
5               <xsd:attribute name="id" type="idDataType"
6                   use="optional"/>
7               <xsd:attribute name="code" type="subfieldcodeDataType"
8                   use="required"/>
9           </xsd:extension>
10      </xsd:simpleContent>
11  </xsd:complexType>
12
13  <xsd:simpleType name="subfieldDataType" id="subfield.st">
14      <xsd:restriction base="xsd:string">
15          <xsd:whiteSpace value="preserve"/>
16      </xsd:restriction>
17  </xsd:simpleType>
18
19  <xsd:simpleType name="subfieldcodeDataType" id="code.st">
20      <xsd:restriction base="xsd:string">
21          <xsd:whiteSpace value="preserve"/>
22          <xsd:pattern value=
23          "[\da-z!&quot;#$%&amp;'()*+,-./:;&lt;=&gt;?{}_^`~\[\]\\]{1}"/>
24      </xsd:restriction>
25  </xsd:simpleType>
26  … …
```

In Fragment 11, the first block of code (lines 2–11) is a complex type definition derived from a base type. It adds two attributes to the base type: the id attribute (optional) and the code attribute (required). Accordingly, with the codes in Fragment 9 and Fragment 10, in an instance document, now you can have this or any similar MARC variable data field.

```
<dataField tag="245" ind1="1" ind2="4">
    <subfield code="...">The little match-seller </subfield>
    <subfield code="...">Hans Christian Andersen</subfield>
</dataField>
```

The code attribute will be used to store a MARC subfield code, which is a data element identifier. There can be three types of values for the identifier:

1. Numeric identifiers are defined for parametric data used to process the field or coded data needed to interpret the field.
2. Alphabetic identifiers are defined for the separate elements that constitute the data content of the field.
3. The character 9 and the following graphic symbols are reserved for local definition as data element identifiers: ! " # $ % & ' ( ) * + ' - . / : ; < = > ?

To implement this, the code attribute has a type with an allowed value that is expressed in regular expression (Fragments 9–20 line 23): [\da-z!"#$%&'()*+,-./:;<=>?{}_^`~\[\]\\]{1} that expresses exactly the same constraints as the above types of identifiers. Note that in the regular expression, it uses character entity references to escape those characters that have special meaning in XML:

- Ampersand sign is represented by &
- Less-than sign is represented <
- Greater-than sign is represented by >
- Quotation mark is represented by "

Based on Fragments 9, 10, and 11, in an instance document, you now can have this or any similar MARC variable data field.

```
<dataField tag="245" ind1="1" ind2="4">
<subfield code="a">The little match-seller </subfield>
   <subfield code="c">Hans Christian Andersen</subfield>
</dataField>
```

10. THE ID ATTRIBUTE

In the code fragments in this section, you can almost always find one or more id attributes. This very popular attribute is for a cataloger to assign a unique ID to any meaningful block of code so that it can be located and retrieved easily if needed. The data type of the attribute is shown in Fragment 12.

Fragment 12: The definition of idDataType

```
… …
<xsd:simpleType name="idDataType" id="id.st">
<xsd:restriction base="xsd:ID"/>
</xsd:simpleType>
… …
```

Basically the code means you can use the xsd:ID type. However, more constraints can be specified later if needed. The xsd:ID type is a built-in type of the W3C XML Schema Language to be used as a unique identifier for an XML document. It has the same constraints as an XML Name. Reread Chapter 3 to review what an XML Name is.

11. THE COMPLETE MARC21 SLIM SCHEMA

The following (file name: "myMARC21SLIM.xsd") is the completed version of the MARC21 SLIM Schema. It combines all the fragments we have discussed—no more, no less—and it is only very slightly different from the official version. If you want to read the original version, visit www.loc.gov/standards/ to locate the schema. However, you may not be able to use an xsi:schemaLocation attribute to point to the file for validation. If you want to use the schema for validation, use a local copy.

Figure 10-6: MARC21 SLIM Schema – filename: "myMARC21SLIM.xsd"

```
<?xml version="1.0"?>
<xsd:schema
	xmlns="http://www.loc.gov/MARC21/slim"
	xmlns:xsd="http://www.w3.org/2001/XMLSchema"
	targetNamespace="http://www.loc.gov/MARC21/slim"
	elementFormDefault="qualified"
	version="1.1"
	xml:lang="en"
>
```

(cont'd.)

Figure 10-6: MARC21 SLIM Schema – filename: "myMARC21SLIM.xsd" ***(Continued)***

```
<!— This is a slightly edited version of the MARC 21 SLIM schema.
The original version is developed and maintained by the Library of Congress, accessible by
http://www.loc.gov/standards/marcxml/schema/MARC21slim.xsd
-->

<xsd:element name="record" type="recordType" nillable="true" id="record.e">
    <xsd:annotation>
        <xsd:documentation>record is a top level container element for all of the field elements which compose
the record</xsd:documentation>
    </xsd:annotation>
</xsd:element>

<xsd:element name="collection" type="collectionType" nillable="true" id="collection.e">
    <xsd:annotation>
        <xsd:documentation>collection is a top level container element for 0 or many records</xsd:documentation>
    </xsd:annotation>
</xsd:element>

<xsd:complexType name="collectionType" id="collection.ct">
    <xsd:sequence minOccurs="0" maxOccurs="unbounded">
        <xsd:element ref="record"/>
    </xsd:sequence>
    <xsd:attribute name="id" type="idDataType" use="optional"/>
</xsd:complexType>

<xsd:complexType name="recordType" id="record.ct">
    <xsd:sequence minOccurs="0">
        <xsd:element name="leader" type="leaderFieldType"/>
        <xsd:element name="controlfield" type="controlFieldType" minOccurs="0" maxOccurs="unbounded"/>
        <xsd:element name="datafield" type="dataFieldType" minOccurs="0" maxOccurs="unbounded"/>
    </xsd:sequence>
    <xsd:attribute name="type" type="recordTypeType" use="optional"/>
    <xsd:attribute name="id" type="idDataType" use="optional"/>
</xsd:complexType>

<xsd:simpleType name="recordTypeType" id="type.st">
    <xsd:restriction base="xsd:NMTOKEN">
        <xsd:enumeration value="Bibliographic"/>
        <xsd:enumeration value="Authority"/>
```

(cont'd.)

Figure 10-6: MARC21 SLIM Schema – filename: "myMARC21SLIM.xsd" ***(Continued)***

```
    <xsd:enumeration value="Holdings"/>
    <xsd:enumeration value="Classification"/>
    <xsd:enumeration value="Community"/>
  </xsd:restriction>
</xsd:simpleType>

<xsd:complexType name="leaderFieldType" id="leader.ct">
  <xsd:annotation>
    <xsd:documentation>MARC21 Leader, 24 bytes</xsd:documentation>
  </xsd:annotation>
  <xsd:simpleContent>
    <xsd:extension base="leaderDataType">
      <xsd:attribute name="id" type="idDataType" use="optional"/>
    </xsd:extension>
  </xsd:simpleContent>
</xsd:complexType>

<xsd:simpleType name="leaderDataType" id="leader.st">
  <xsd:restriction base="xsd:string">
    <xsd:whiteSpace value="preserve"/>
    <xsd:pattern value="[\d ]{5}[\dA-Za-z ]{1}[\dA-Za-z]{1}[\dA-Za-z ]{3}(2| )(2| )[\d ]{5}[\dA-Za-z ]{3}(4500| )"/>
  </xsd:restriction>
</xsd:simpleType>

<xsd:complexType name="controlFieldType" id="controlfield.ct">
  <xsd:annotation>
    <xsd:documentation>MARC21 Fields 001-009</xsd:documentation>
  </xsd:annotation>
  <xsd:simpleContent>
    <xsd:extension base="controlDataType">
      <xsd:attribute name="id" type="idDataType" use="optional"/>
      <xsd:attribute name="tag" type="controltagDataType" use="required"/>
    </xsd:extension>
  </xsd:simpleContent>
</xsd:complexType>

<xsd:simpleType name="controlDataType" id="controlfield.st">
  <xsd:restriction base="xsd:string">
```

(cont'd.)

Figure 10-6: MARC21 SLIM Schema – filename: "myMARC21SLIM.xsd" *(Continued)*

```
        <xsd:whiteSpace value="preserve"/>
    </xsd:restriction>
</xsd:simpleType>

<xsd:simpleType name="controltagDataType" id="controltag.st">
    <xsd:restriction base="xsd:string">
        <xsd:whiteSpace value="preserve"/>
        <xsd:pattern value="00[1-9A-Za-z]{1}"/>
    </xsd:restriction>
</xsd:simpleType>

<xsd:complexType name="dataFieldType" id="datafield.ct">
    <xsd:annotation>
        <xsd:documentation>MARC21 Variable Data Fields 010-999 </xsd:documentation>
    </xsd:annotation>
    <xsd:sequence maxOccurs="unbounded">
        <xsd:element name="subfield" type="subfielddatafieldType"/>
    </xsd:sequence>
    <xsd:attribute name="id" type="idDataType" use="optional"/>
    <xsd:attribute name="tag" type="tagDataType" use="required"/>
    <xsd:attribute name="ind1" type="indicatorDataType" use="required"/>
<xsd:attribute name="ind2" type="indicatorDataType" use="required"/>
</xsd:complexType>

<xsd:simpleType name="tagDataType" id="tag.st">
    <xsd:restriction base="xsd:string">
        <xsd:whiteSpace value="preserve"/>
            <xsd:pattern value="(0([1-9A-Z][0-9A-Z])|0([1-9a-z][0-9a-z]))|(([1-9A-Z][0-9A-Z]{2})|([1-9a-z]
                                [0-9a-z]{2}))"/>
    </xsd:restriction>
</xsd:simpleType>

<xsd:simpleType name="indicatorDataType" id="ind.st">
    <xsd:restriction base="xsd:string">
        <xsd:whiteSpace value="preserve"/>
        <xsd:pattern value="[\da-z ]{1}"/>
    </xsd:restriction>
</xsd:simpleType>
```

(cont'd.)

Figure 10-6: MARC21 SLIM Schema – filename: "myMARC21SLIM.xsd" ***(Continued)***

```
<xsd:complexType name="subfieldatafieldType" id="subfield.ct">
    <xsd:simpleContent>
        <xsd:extension base="subfieldDataType">
            <xsd:attribute name="id" type="idDataType" use="optional"/>
            <xsd:attribute name="code" type="subfieldcodeDataType" use="required"/>
        </xsd:extension>
    </xsd:simpleContent>
</xsd:complexType>

<xsd:simpleType name="subfieldDataType" id="subfield.st">
    <xsd:restriction base="xsd:string">
        <xsd:whiteSpace value="preserve"/>
    </xsd:restriction>
</xsd:simpleType>

<xsd:simpleType name="subfieldcodeDataType" id="code.st">
    <xsd:restriction base="xsd:string">
        <xsd:whiteSpace value="preserve"/>
            <xsd:pattern value="[\da-z!&quot;#$%&amp;'()*+,-./:;&lt;=&gt;?{}_^`~\[\]\\]{1}"/>
    </xsd:restriction>
</xsd:simpleType>

<xsd:simpleType name="idDataType" id="id.st">
    <xsd:restriction base="xsd:ID"/>
</xsd:simpleType>

</xsd:schema>
```

12. USING THE SCHEMA

The following are two records using the MARC21 SLIM Schema. The first is a bibliographic record. The second is a name-author record for H. C. Andersen. Both of them are created by the author of this book for demonstration purpose only.

Figure 10-7: A Bibliographic Catalog Using the MARC21 SLIM Schema – filename: "bibRec.xml"

```
<?xml version="1.0" encoding="UTF-8"?>
<collection xmlns="http://www.loc.gov/MARC21/slim"
      xmlns:xsi="http://www.w3.org/2001/XMLSchema-instance"
      xsi:schemaLocation="http://www.loc.gov/MARC21/slim  myMARC21SLIM.xsd">
   <record type="Bibliographic">
      <leader>01112cam 22003301a 4500</leader>
      <controlfield tag="001">4752360</controlfield>
      <controlfield tag="003">DLC</controlfield>
      <controlfield tag="005">19881203231624.0</controlfield>
      <controlfield tag="008">851206s1987 ccua j 000 1 eng</controlfield>
      <datafield tag="010" ind1=" " ind2=" ">
         <subfield code="a">85530982</subfield>
      </datafield>
      <datafield tag="020" ind1=" " ind2=" ">
         <subfield code="a">0399413768 :</subfield>
         <subfield code="c">$13.95</subfield>
      </datafield>
      <datafield tag="020" ind1=" " ind2=" ">
         <subfield code="a">0399217376 (pbk.) :</subfield>
         <subfield code="c">$18.95</subfield>
      </datafield>
      <datafield tag="040" ind1=" " ind2=" ">
         <subfield code="a">DLC</subfield>
         <subfield code="c">DLC</subfield>
         <subfield code="d">DLC</subfield>
      </datafield>
      <datafield tag="041" ind1="1" ind2=" ">
         <subfield code="a">eng</subfield>
         <subfield code="h">dan</subfield>
      </datafield>
      <datafield tag="042" ind1=" " ind2=" ">
         <subfield code="a">lcac</subfield>
      </datafield>
      <datafield tag="050" ind1="0" ind2="0">
         <subfield code="a">PZ8.A542</subfield>
         <subfield code="b">1987</subfield>
      </datafield>
      <datafield tag="082" ind1="0" ind2="0">
```

(cont'd.)

Figure 10-7: A Bibliographic Catalog Using the MARC 21 SLIM Schema – filename: "bibRec.xml" ***(Continued)***


```
      <subfield code="a">[Fic]</subfield>
      <subfield code="2">19</subfield>
    </datafield>
    <datafield tag="100" ind1="1" ind2=" ">
      <subfield code="a">Andersen, H.C.</subfield>
      <subfield code="q">(Hans Christian),</subfield>
      <subfield code="d">1805-1875.</subfield>
    </datafield>
    <datafield tag="240" ind1="1" ind2="0">
      <subfield code="a">Lille pige med svovlstikkerne.</subfield>
      <subfield code="l">English</subfield>
    </datafield>
    <datafield tag="245" ind1="1" ind2="4">
      <subfield code="a">The little match-seller /</subfield>
      <subfield code="c">Hans Christian Andersen</subfield>
    </datafield>
    <datafield tag="260" ind1=" " ind2=" ">
      <subfield code="a">New York :</subfield>
      <subfield code="b">ABCDE Publisher,</subfield>
      <subfield code="c">c1984.</subfield>
    </datafield>
    <datafield tag="300" ind1=" " ind2=" ">
      <subfield code="a">50 p. :</subfield>
      <subfield code="b">col. ill. ;</subfield>
      <subfield code="c">24 x 29 cm.</subfield>
    </datafield>
    <datafield tag="500" ind1=" " ind2=" ">
      <subfield code="a">Translation of: Lille pige med svovlstikkerne.</subfield>
    </datafield>
    <datafield tag="520" ind1=" " ind2=" ">
      <subfield code="a">Sad story of a poor little match seller girl who lives on the streets,
succumbs to freezing cold weather, tries to warm up by lighting her matches. Then she enters a
fantastic world of dreams. The following morning, she is found frozen and dead.</subfield>
    </datafield>
    <datafield tag="650" ind1=" " ind2="1">
      <subfield code="a">Fairy tales.</subfield>
    </datafield>
  </record>
</collection>
```

Figure 10-8: An Authority Record Using the MARC21 SLIM Schema – filename: "autRec.xml"

```
<?xml version="1.0" encoding="UTF-8"?>
<collection xmlns="http://www.loc.gov/MARC21/slim"
        xmlns:xsi="http://www.w3.org/2001/XMLSchema-instance"
        xsi:schemaLocation="http://www.loc.gov/MARC21/slim
            myMARC21SLIM.xsd">
    <record type="Authority">
                <leader>00433cz    2200245n   4500</leader>
            <controlfield tag="001">n   00806108 </controlfield>
            <controlfield tag="003">DLC</controlfield>
            <controlfield tag="005">20050301151458.0</controlfield>
            <controlfield tag="008">001027n| acannaabn           |a aaa </controlfield>
            <datafield tag="010" ind1=" " ind2=" ">
                <subfield code="a">n 00908108 </subfield>
            </datafield>
            <datafield tag="035" ind1=" " ind2=" ">
                <subfield code="a">(OCoLC)oca06391508</subfield>
            </datafield>
            <datafield tag="040" ind1=" " ind2=" ">
                <subfield code="a">DLC</subfield>
                <subfield code="b">eng</subfield>
                <subfield code="c">DLC</subfield>
                <subfield code="d">DLC</subfield>
                <subfield code="d">WaU</subfield>
            </datafield>
            <datafield tag="100" ind1="1" ind2=" ">
                <subfield code="a">Andersen, H. C.</subfield>
            </datafield>
            <datafield tag="400" ind1="1" ind2=" ">
                <subfield code="a">Walter, Villiam Christian</subfield>
            </datafield>
        </record>
</collection>
```

3 APPENDIX 3: GLOSSARY — SOME BASIC XML TERMS

ASP: ASP stands for Active Server Pages. It is a technology created by Microsoft for server-side programming. Usually it is used to dynamically generate Web pages.

Attribute: In XML, an attribute provides more information about an element. It is used to associate name-value pairs with elements.

CDATA: CDATA is an XML keyword for character data that should not be parsed, as opposed to "Parsed Character Data" (PCDATA). See also PCDATA.

CSS: Cascading Style Sheets (CSS) is a language used for attaching style (e.g., fonts, spacing, and aural cues) to structured documents (e.g., HTML documents and XML applications). CSS Level 1 became a World Wide Web Consortium (W3C) recommendation in 1996 and was revised in 1999. CSS Level 2 was built on CSS Level 1. It became a World Wide Web Consortium (W3C) recommendation in 1998. CSS Level 2 also supports content positioning, downloadable fonts, table layout, features for internationalization, automatic counters and numbering, and some properties related to user interface.

DCMES: DCMES (Dublin Core Metadata Element Set) is a vocabulary of 15 metadata elements for use in cross-domain resource description. Its primary purpose is to facilitate discovery of all kinds of electronic resources. For more information, please visit: http://dublincore.org/documents/dces/

DCMI: DCMI stands for the Dublin Core Metadata Initiative, which is an open organization engaged in the development of interoperable online metadata standards that support a broad range of purposes and business models. For more information, please visit: http://dublincore.org/

Declaration: A declaration in an XML document is a statement declaring the existence of a document type, an element, an attribute, an entity, or a namespace that will be used or referenced to in the body of document.

DTD: Document Type Definition (DTD) describes the structure of a document written in XML or SGML. XML DTD is the formal definition that specifies the elements, attributes, entities, and comments for a class of XML documents. You can store a DTD at the beginning of a document or externally in a separate file.

EAD: Encoded Archival Description (EAD) is a standard for encoding archival finding aids using Extensible Markup Language (XML). The standard is maintained in the Network Development and MARC Standards Office of the Library of Congress (LC) in partnership with the Society of American Archivists (SAA).

Element: Element is a structural construct of XML. It is the basic building unit of an XML document. It includes a start tag, an end tag, and a piece data enclosed by the tags. Usually we call the enclosed data the content of the element. For example, <Author>Kwong Bor Ng</Author> can be an XML element, with <Author> as the start tag, </Author> as the end tag, and Kwong Bor Ng as the content of the element.

Entity: An entity in an XML document is a self-contained piece of data that can be referenced as a unit. An entity can be a string of characters, a symbol character (that is unavailable on a standard keyboard), a separate text file, or a separate graphic file.

GML: Generator Markup Language (GML) is the language developed by IBM for integrated text processing. It was the first markup language attempted to use formally defined document type for grammar specification. It laid down the foundation for the development of SGML and XML.

MADS: Metadata Authority Description Schema (MADS) is a MARC21-compatible XML format for the type of data carried in records in the MARC Authorities format. It is used to provide metadata about agents (people, organizations), events, and terms (topics, geographic points, genres, etc.). The standard is developed and maintained by the Network Development and MARC Standards Office of the Library of Congress with input from users.

MARC and MARC21: MAchine-Readable Cataloging (MARC) is a data format used by libraries to store and exchange catalog records. It provides the mechanism by which computers exchange, use, and interpret bibliographic information. MARC became USMARC in the 1980s and MARC21 in the late 1990s.

Markup: Markup is anything added to the content of a document that describes the text. A document encoded in a markup language consists of markup tags intermingled with the primary text. The best-known markup language in modern use is HTML (HyperText Markup Language).

METS: Metadata Encoding & Transmission Standard (METS) is a standard for encoding descriptive, administrative, and structural metadata regarding objects within a digital library, expressed using the W3C

XML Schema Language. The standard is maintained in the Network Development and MARC Standards Office of the Library of Congress, and is being developed as an initiative of the Digital Library Federation.

MODS: Metadata Object Description Schema (MODS) is an XML schema for a bibliographic element set that may be used for a variety of purposes, and particularly for library applications. It is expressed using the W3C XML Schema Language. The standard is maintained by the Network Development and MARC Standards Office of the Library of Congress.

Namespace: An XML namespace is a collection of names used in XML documents as element types and attribute names. In XML, there is a simple method for qualifying element and attribute names used in XML documents by associating them with their namespaces identified by URI or URL references.

NISO: The National Information Standards Organization (NISO) is an association accredited by the American National Standards Institute. It identifies, develops, maintains, and publishes technical standards to manage information in digital environment. NISO standards apply both traditional and new technologies to the full range of information-related needs, including retrieval, re-purposing, storage, metadata, and preservation.

Parser: An XML parser is a specialized software program that recognizes XML markup in a document. It reads XML DTDs and XML schemas in order to format a conforming XML document accordingly. A parser can be built into an XML editor to prevent incorrect tagging and to check whether a document contains all the required elements.

Pattern (in XSLT): In XSLT, a language for transforming XML documents from one format to another, transformation rules should only be applied to the intended parts (nodes) of an XML document. The intended parts are identified using pattern. A pattern specifies a set of conditions that needed to be satisfied for a particular set of transforming rules to apply. If the conditions are satisfied, we say there is a match between the pattern and the node. For example, the pattern text() will match any element that has only textual data but no child elements as its content.

PCDATA: PCDATA means Parsed Character Data. It is the text that will be parsed by an XML parser. Tags inside the text will be treated as markup, and entities will be expanded to their replacement texts.

PHP: Hypertext Preprocessor (PHP) is one of the most popular server-side scripting languages for the Web environment. It is used primarily for processing data at the server-side and creating dynamic content that will be delivered over the Internet and rendered by a Web browser at the client side.

Qualified Dublin Core: Each of the 15 Dublin Core Metadata Elements (see DCMI and DCMES) can be associated with some qualifiers to refine the meaning of a resource or to specify the encoding scheme used. For example, to specify that you are using the DCMES element "Title" to refer to a specific kind of title, "alternative title," you can associate the qualifier "alternative" with "Title" in your record. The actual mechanism of association qualifier to DCMES depends on the encoding scheme you use. For more information, please visit: http://dublincore.org/documents/usageguide/qualifiers.shtml

RDF: Resource Description Framework (RDF) is a general framework for describing resources accessible on the Internet. RDF is designed to represent information in a minimally constraining, flexible way. Many Dublin Core Metadata records of online resources were created in RDF format.

Regular expression: In various computer languages, regular expression refers to a set of symbols and syntax to express conditions on a string of character data. Usually it is used to search and match text for further processing. For example, in the W3C XML Schema Language, the regular expression \d (i.e., a slash followed immediate by the lower case letter d) matches any textual string that has a numeric digit in it.

Relax NG: RELAX NG (REgular LAnguage for XML Next Generation) is a schema language for XML. Compared to other popular schema languages, like W3C's XML Schema Language, RELAX NG is relatively simpler.

Schema: XML Schema is a mechanism for describing the structure and constraining the contents of XML documents. It can be expressed in several different schema languages, e.g., the W3C XML Schema Language, the RELAX NG (RELAX New Generation) language, etc.

SGML: Standard Generalized Markup Language (SGML) is a general-purpose markup language for creating special markup languages. It can be used to organize and tag elements to describe information embedded within a document. SGML was developed and standardized by the International Organization for Standards (ISO).

Simple Content and Complex Content: In the W3C XML Schema language, an element is said to have complex type if it contains child element(s) or attribute(s). If a complex type element has only attributes and no child element, it has simple content. If a complex type element has child element(s), whether it has attributes or not, it has complex content.

Simple Type and Complex Type: In the W3C XML Schema Language, an XML element that contains child elements or carries attributes is said to have complex types, whereas elements that contain numbers, strings, and dates, etc., but do not contain any sub-elements are said to have simple types.

SVG: Scalable Vector Graphics (SVG) is a language for describing two-dimensional graphics and graphical applications in XML. It can be used to describe three types of graphic objects: vector graphic shapes (e.g., paths consisting of straight lines and curves), images, and text.

TEI: Text Encoding Initiative (TEI) Guidelines represent an international and interdisciplinary standard that enables libraries, museums, publishers, and individual scholars to represent a variety of literary and linguistic texts for online research, teaching, and preservation. It was originally sponsored by the Association of Computers in the Humanities, the Association for Computational Linguistics, and the Association of Literary and Linguistic Computing. The past few versions of TEI were expressed in XML DTD format. The newest version (P5) switches from XML DTD to XML Schema.

Valid: A valid XML document is a well-formed XML document, with a document structure that also conforms to a set of formal constraints expressed either in DTD or in schema. See also Well-formed, DTD, and Schema.

W3C Consortium and W3C Recommendations: World Wide Web Consortium (W3C) is an international consortium for developing Web standards. Its mission is "to lead the World Wide Web to its full potential by developing protocols and guidelines that ensure long-term growth for the Web." W3C primarily pursues its mission through the creation of Web standards and guidelines, which are published as W3C Recommendations.

Well-formed: An XML document must be well formed. A well-formed XML document is one that meets the minimal set of criteria for it to be a correct XML document. Some of the most basic criteria are: (1) it must have a root element; (2) all elements must have start tags and end tags (except empty elements which can use a special short format); (3) all elements are properly nested; and (4) attribute values are quoted. XML processors will not process any XML document that is not well formed.

XML: XML (Extensible Markup Language) is a general purpose markup language that allows information, data, and metadata to be encoded with meaningful structure and semantics that computers and humans can understand. It is a simplified subset of the Standardized Generalized Markup Language (SGML) that provides a file format for representing data. It allows authors to define their own tags and their own document structure.

XML name: A name in XML can be an element name, attribute name, processing instruction target, entity name, or a notation name. It is a token beginning with a letter or one of a few punctuation characters and continuing with letters, digits, hyphens, underscores, colons, or full stops, together known as name characters. Names beginning with the string "xml," or with any string that would match (('X'|'x') ('M'|'m') ('L'|'l')) are reserved for standardization and should not be used.

XPath: When writing code to process XML, you often want to select specific parts of an XML document to process in a particular way. XPath is a language primarily for addressing parts of an XML document. It also provides basic facilities for manipulation of strings, numbers and Booleans (i.e., data type that has only two possible values, e.g., yes or no, 0 or 1, etc.). You can use it to navigate through elements and attributes of an XML document to locate information.

XSL: Extensible Style Language (XSL) is a family of W3C recommendations for defining XML document transformation and presentation. It consists of three parts: (1) XSL Transformations (XSLT), a language for transforming XML; (2) the XML Path Language (XPath), an expression language used by XSLT to access or refer to parts of an XML document; and (3) XSL Formatting Objects (XSL-FO), an XML vocabulary for specifying formatting semantics.

XSL-FO: XSL Formatting Objects (XSL-FO) is an XML markup language for document formatting. It is can be used to specify physical layout, coloring, typography, etc., of XML documents for screen, print, and other media.

XSLT: Extensible Style Sheet Transformations (XSLT) is a language for transforming an XML document. It is itself a dialect of XML. An XSLT style sheet specifies the presentation of a class of XML documents by describing how an instance of the class is transformed into an XML document that uses a formatting vocabulary.

URI and URL: Uniform Resource Identifier (URI) is an Internet protocol element consisting of a short string of characters. The string comprises a name or address that can be used to refer to a resource. It is a fundamental component of the World Wide Web. For example, the Web address of a Web site is called a URL (Uniform Resource Locator), which is a subset of URI.

APPENDIX 4: TABLE OF COMMON NUMERIC REFERENCES

Table of Common Numeric References		
Character	**Hexadecimal character reference**	**Decimal character reference**
¡	¡	¡
¢	¢	¢
£	£	£
¥	¥	¥
¦	¦	¦
§	§	§
©	©	©
¬	¬	¬
®	®	®
°	°	°
±	±	±
´	´	´
_	µ	µ
¶	¶	¶
¼	¼	¼
½	½	½
¾	¾	¾
¿	¿	¿
À	À	À
Á	Á	Á
		(cont'd.)

Table of Common Numeric References ***(Continued)***

Character	Hexadecimal character reference	Decimal character reference
Ã	Ã	Ã
Ä	Ä	Ä
Å	Å	Å
Æ	Æ	Æ
Ç	Ç	Ç
È	È	È
É	É	É
Ê	Ê	Ê
Ë	Ë	Ë
Ì	Ì	Ì
Í	Í	Í
Î	Î	Î
Ï	Ï	Ï
Ñ	Ñ	Ñ
Ò	Ò	Ò
Ó	Ó	Ó
Ô	Ô	Ô
Õ	Õ	Õ
Ö	Ö	Ö
Ø	Ø	Ø
Ù	Ù	Ù
Ú	Ú	Ú
Û	Û	Û
Ü	Ü	Ü
ß	ß	ß
à	à	à

(cont'd.)

Table of Common Numeric References *(Continued)*		
Character	**Hexadecimal character reference**	**Decimal character reference**
á	á	á
â	â	â
ã	ã	ã
ä	ä	ä
å	å	å
æ	æ	æ
ç	ç	ç
è	è	è
é	é	é
ê	ê	ê
ë	ë	ë
ì	ì	ì
í	í	í
î	î	î
ï	ï	ï
ñ	ñ	ñ
ò	ò	ò
ó	ó	ó
ô	ô	ô
õ	õ	õ
ö	ö	ö
÷	÷	÷
ù	ù	ù
ú	ú	ú
û	û	û
ü	ü	ü

(cont'd.)

Table of Common Numeric References *(Continued)*		
Character	**Hexadecimal character reference**	**Decimal character reference**
ÿ	ÿ	ÿ
"	"	"
&	&	&
'	'	'
<	<	<
>	>	>
~	ˆ	ˆ
-	–	–
-	—	—
`	‘	‘
_	μ	μ
...	…	…
/	⁄	⁄
™	™	™
*	∗	∗

INDEX

ABOUT THE AUTHOR

Kwong Bor Ng (Ph.D.) is an associate professor at the Graduate School of Library and Information Studies of Queens College, CUNY. He is also a consultant for various research projects sponsored by the National Science Foundation. His research interests are in the technical and technological areas of knowledge representation and organization. At Queens College, he teaches courses on XML, information visualization, database construction, as well as cataloging and classification.